D · H · LAWRENCE

A First Study

Also by STEPHEN POTTER
The Young Man
A novel

D. H. LAWRENCE
1929

D·H·LAWRENCE

A First Study

by

STEPHEN POTTER

London · JONATHAN CAPE · Toronto
JONATHAN CAPE & HARRISON SMITH
New York

FIRST PUBLISHED 1930

JONATHAN CAPE 30 BEDFORD SQUARE LONDON
& 77 WELLINGTON STREET WEST, TORONTO
JONATHAN CAPE & HARRISON SMITH
139 EAST 46TH STREET NEW YORK

PRINTED IN GREAT BRITAIN BY
THE GARDEN CITY PRESS LTD
LETCHWORTH

CONTENTS

6 CONTENTS

PART FOUR
SOME CONCLUSIONS

APPENDIX

PORTRAITS

NOTE ON
THE PORTRAITS

1. The frontispiece is a photograph taken in the spring of 1929.

2. The photograph facing page 38 was taken on Lawrence's twenty-first birthday. In answer to a question, Lawrence wrote of the existence of this portrait which showed him, he said, as a 'clean-shaven, bright young prig in a high collar like a curate, guaranteed to counteract all the dark and sinister effect of all the newspaper photographs.'
For permission to reproduce this portrait of her brother I am greatly indebted to the kindness of Mrs. King.

3. The drawing facing page 94 is a self-portrait done in 1929.

'The artist usually sets out – or used to – to point a moral and adorn a tale. The tale, however, points the other way, as a rule. Two blankly opposing morals, the artist's and the tale's. Never trust the artist. Trust the tale. The proper function of a critic is to save the tale from the artist who created it.'
— *Studies in Classic American Literature*

INTRODUCTION

LAWRENCE died on the 3rd of March, 1930, when these pages were in proof. Although what I have written deals largely with the autobiographical side of his work, the book is not a biography but a comment on certain aspects of his writings, so that with the exception of this opening paragraph and the closing lines I have made no alteration. It has been impossible to obey the impulse to cut out some of the less essential criticisms which in the realisation of the fact of his death have seemed half irrelevant.

I call this book a first study for two reasons. First because it seems strange that although he has been the subject of so many references, often important, from writers as far apart as Wyndham Lewis and Middleton Murry, E. M. Forster and T. S. Eliot, Arnold Bennett and the reviewers of the *New Statesman*, yet there has been, so far, no book published in England with D. H. Lawrence as its main subject. Perhaps it is that those who think him bad think him so bad as not to be worth writing about, and those who think him good think him so good that the fear of unworthiness goes the other way. The greater part of Lawrence's public however comes from neither of these two classes. The majority of his readers are youngish, normally educated, somewhat conventional men who, attracted by hearsay knowledge of Lawrence as a breaker down of established things, have made use of him, or have naturally taken to him, as a means to make their own continued growth easier.

The relation which such a 'minority man,' such an attacker of established values, establishes with young admirers is sometimes described as that of a spiritual father. This term remarkably fails to fit Lawrence (it is more applicable, for instance, to Bernard Shaw, who has been the spiritual father to numbers of men who were in their twenties before the war). But whatever it is which is being broken down, it is always the iconoclasm of these pioneers that makes them read by young men, and it is the iconoclasm which they will need and use: as Shaw himself used Butler; as Goethe used Shakespeare [1] ; as Carlyle and Walter Scott used Goethe. And the studies of the young men will always be accompanied by passionate admiration, not for the phenomenon of their growth, but for these instruments by means of which they have freed themselves.

Yet when the young men come to read these former heroes afterwards, the direction of their growth having meanwhile perhaps entirely changed, all the attacks and conquests made will seem rather meaningless and unnecessary. Disappointment – but now comes the test of the breaker of images, the permanence of whose influence will depend on what he has set up in their place.

Unless, then, the subject is to be *Lawrence as Historical Phenomenon*, the question chiefly worth discussing is what is there *besides* the wonderfully ener-

---

[1] i.e. to break from the French tradition.

getic scrapping which is the obvious and famous thing about most of Lawrence's work? This book, by one of the typical Lawrence readers already described, is an attempt to make this estimate.

It is written without the help of personal knowledge – or would it be the hindrance? In personal meetings I am so often conscious of being too much taken up by the human side both of the stranger and still more of myself for there to be much meeting in it at all. Lawrence is a man of strong personality – strong character, and this book is written to show my contact not so much with this character, so obvious in his books, but with Lawrence himself.

Of course there is the hearsay of English friends. Yet it is really no good being told that Lawrence is fastidious about food, talks at great length, nor even that he has weak lungs, but that his body has apparently endless powers of resistence and recuperation. This might come out of any last chapter of the old *English Men of Letters*. Nor that his walk is slinking like a Hindu's – I don't believe this: nor that in England he was noted for being rude to women who sang songs at the piano after dinner. This might be true of any would-be ruthless genius. And it is certainly no good looking at snaps of Lawrence taken in England when he was thirty by friends at picnics, showing Lawrence with cavernous eyes, a dark beard encroaching high on his cheeks, and thick dark hair. Base a chapter on the symbolical significance of this racial darkness if you like, but in actual fact his beard is red. And mannerism – even characteristics – may be more misleading than photographs, so I do not regret the lack of personal knowledge so much.

Nevertheless apart from the personal gap this is a first study, and if its author and its subject are still living in five years, the estimate of Lawrence which it contains would be so thoroughly superseded that a further and better one might be written. This present book must, by the limitations of its nature, leave a great deal to be said.

PART ONE
NERI AND BIANCI

NERI AND BIANCI

LAWRENCE'S REPUTATION. Lawrence is famous. The peak year of his reputation was 1921, after the publication of *Women in Love*, since when his name among the intelligentsia – I wish there was an uncynical name for them – has lost value. This has synchronised, however, with a growing newspaper fame, and the acquiring of a definite newspaper character: i.e. he is showing signs of stepping into Bernard Shaw's shoes as a 'fearless,' stop-at-nothing, trenchant, and above all bannable young writer. Now, his public character decided, it is established and filled out exclusively by news of Lawrence which fits this conception.

No one is surprised, therefore, on reading 'Indecent Manuscripts Seized in Post,' to hear that the author who has written an angry letter of complaint is D. H. Lawrence. When the 'Police Raid Picture Gallery,' perhaps few guess the identity of the artist – until they hear that some of the pictures give prominence to the sexual organs. Even when, as on this occasion, the police, thinking rightly that there was something queer about the whole place, went back for a further search to find, sure enough, that there was a whole pile of drawings – nudes – not by Lawrence but signed 'Wm. Blake,' and when, the date having triumphantly made all decent, the business closed in general laughter – even this led to a vague heightening of Lawrence's public reputation though in point of fact the pictures were of small value.[1]

This is an unwieldy kind of fame for Lawrence to have acquired. It may partly explain why it is that in England at any rate he is not proportionately widely read. For every one person who reads his books there are ten who understand that what he writes has generally something to do with *sex*, that he speaks often of the *unconscious*, that he uses the word *dark* as often as Dante uses the word *light*, and that he believes in the importance of savages, animals, and the Holy Ghost.

This is the 'point about Lawrence' according to those who read books 'critically.' To some this means running quickly through the pages to pick out bits which are consistent with each other or with a general map of the writer drawn from hearsay. Francis Bacon calls this a fallacious method of judgment: *Inductio per enumerationem simplicem* — taking exclusively the cases which happen to support a particular theory. But it is only fallacious if the author has something more than ideas to his book. It is all very well to say that books should be read for inconsistencies, that the reader should lose himself, so that the knowledge expressed by the writer which corresponds to unexpressed knowledge in himself can join on naturally and not be painstakingly fixed to the outside. If the book only contains detached ideas, it doesn't particularly matter which are chosen.

[1] I regret I am not speaking from first-hand knowledge.

But if there is something more, then the gist alone is meaningless. It makes Lawrence meaningless, I believe, to read him for his 'points.' Skipping through the descriptive passages, good as they are, of course, to see what he says about sex and savages. And after all even the sex parts are not nearly so fascinating as Havelock Ellis nor as startling as Freud used to be; and they have none of the marvellous detachment of Proust. Really he is quite *vieux jeu*.

It is perfectly true. Lawrence is *vieux jeu*, and it is his own fault. Part of his work was *vieux jeu* the moment he had written it, for Lawrence is a writer with a philosophy.

WRITERS WITH A PHILOSOPHY. During all his writing life Lawrence has had a philosophy, and he has been true to it. But the philosophy has not always been true to him. A metaphysic is either a comment on experience, in which case it has only absolute truth at the moment of its formulation. Or it is a dogma evolved from dogmas, in which case it is either pure academicism, or has truth only as the expression of a hatred, an attack on some part of life which the writer has failed to acknowledge.

Such a philosophy, therefore, is always the least valuable part of an author's work. It is a record of what he has failed to experience, and the world he has to present is a created one only in so far as it is not obscured by the scheme attached. Interesting

B

as it is to codify these dogmatic beliefs, it is far more
important to disentangle a writer from the metaphysic which hides him. In the case of some
writers this sifting is unnecessary. Whitman, for
instance – Goethe the same. 'Everything fits in
because I have no system,' he wrote. But the saying
should be reversed. Because everything fitted in,
because there was nothing he avoided, nothing
which, by having failed to experience it through
and through, he passionately resented – for that
reason he was able not to have a system.

Sometimes, on the other hand, the bars of the
philosophic cage are so close set that the author
himself can never be got at. This is not the case
with Lawrence. But there is enough moralisation
to obscure, with the help of this fixed public reputation of his, a great deal of what is good in him:
and interesting as it is to discuss the hatreds and
revulsions which are responsible for this 'gist' of
his work, this section is put first for the sake of
clarity; it is not first in importance.

HATREDS. Freudian psychology, going not so much
to the root of the matter as to the base of one of the
offshoots, would put everything down to the 'father.'
Lawrence was born[1] in a Midland coal district –
Eastwood in Nottinghamshire – and his father was
a miner, with no pretensions, no pride in respecta-
bility, half-educated, a formidable drinker, slightly

[1] 1885.

brutal, sullen. Lawrence's mother was 'superior.'
She was charmingly different, contained, a lady.
Lawrence himself was a second son; he was often
ill, but forward and very clever. He was against his
father. He despised him and his bad pit manners
and pit dirt. Lawrence grew into an intelligent and
'advanced' youth. He and his mother formed a sort
of league against the 'bad husband.' Lawrence
took his father's place in her regard, and there was
very much of a husband-wife relationship between
them.

Lawrence was a boy of great ambition and
aspiration. His mother increased this by encour-
agement, his father by indifference and by representing his home and way of life as something to
be aspired away from. His father slowly spelt out
the Sunday newspapers: Lawrence learnt languages,
and read advanced books.

Then for a long time, through most of his teens,
he was the companion of a girl about his own age.
This friendship helped him in what he wanted to
be – the girl was herself intense and aspiring, a
passionate Christian, and full of knowledge and
book-reading and emancipation at the same time.
Her everyday life in her own home, too, was one
not to be thought about – the muddiest farm jobs,
and endless washings-up after the big farmhouse
meals. She was carefully self-educated, and interested in movements and ideas; she admired the
promise in Lawrence, meaning by promise something Shelley-like and spiritual, flattering Lawrence,

and making him be half Shelley-like himself to live up to what she saw in him. Lawrence, sure of himself already as a boy of something more than promise, felt that in the teeth of this unpropitious environment of squalor by which they were both handicapped he could fiercely enjoy living a different, ideal life with the girl. They could together think of Beauty, and of how different the world might be made.

Soon Lawrence was at the provincial university, with other young men. There everyone who was worth anything seemed to know that to be Shelley-like and aspiring was right: not to be so was wrong. University education is what young men want it to be and what young men feel as adolescents to be right is what the atmosphere and teaching of universities become. Lawrence found that here the attitude to life was uniform. He found a world where idealism, in the famous nineteenth-century sense, was taken for granted. He found concepts such as Progress: Mankind: the Perfectibility of Man: advanced Politics: the Beauty of Nature — all taken as having absolute truth. He was introduced into a society where certain things, certain people, are taken as being for ever good or for ever bad, according to whether or no they pass the test of kindness, tolerance, unbeast-like look-your-man-in-the-eye straightforwardness. He found, too, that the actual education, the actual studies, were of one certain kind, all taking these standards for granted, all arranged in terms of standards generally, rather than of persons. And in spite of his idealism, he was beginning to find actual persons absorbingly interesting. Yet he discovered, for instance, that in this world, new to him, the study of history was not made to lead to the knowledge of persons who have lived, nor of persons who have created particular historical metaphors, so much as to movements and outlines. That study subjects with titles such as Literature placed writers in some mysterious order of absolute merit, persons who really revealed themselves in writing being placed alongside famous word artists and wits (Coleridge, Juvenal and Froissart bracketed twelfth). Even with a subject so rooted in life as theology, there was the same business of movements and cold historical treatment. Goodness, what a lot of Mithraism there is in early Christianity. And just think of the way ancient Mongol beliefs work into the Orthodox ritual. Really all religions are the same, especially if they happen to be studied quite apart from the persons, the creating persons, in whose track they each separately congealed. Lawrence began to doubt. And all these studies really simply went to prove the marvellous way in which everything is the same. And the atmosphere of the whole thing was – well, not sweetness and light so much as sharp common sense and freedom from cant. For were not such monosyllables as *shaw* and *wells* somewhere in the background, unacademic as they seemed to be? How fresh and jolly the words were – what sanity – what amusements. How magni-

ficent when contrasted with the Victorian suffoca-
tions they arose from. How true and right when
they speak of Jesus, of children, of cruelty. How
unafraid to name bestiality when it appears. . . .

Did this world suit Lawrence now he came to
know it better? He knew himself to be an extraordinary young man; but to push to high ideals was
the rule here, not the exception. Everyone else had
arrived so easily at the conclusions he himself had
worked to step by step. What was the good of being
emancipated if everyone else was emancipated too?
A dogma of emancipation. Lawrence began to feel
a strong repulsion.

Moreover he felt he was being pushed into something. It is not the way of life itself so much as the
determination to impose this way of life which those
who have been hurt by it fear most. Not so much
the passion for sweetness and light as *'the passion
for making them prevail'* italicised by Arnold.

He might have appraised and really got to know
this curious world. He might have made it part of
his own. But he could not. He could not manage
it. The most difficult thing for a young man to
accept is the way of life which is about him when
he begins the final and most important stage of
growth. Lawrence could not: he could not engulf
it. But he was very far from being engulfed by it.
He was not going to wander 'between two worlds,
one dead, the other powerless to be born.' In a
life which he began to think of as full of a dead
mode of living, what he did was to turn against

his dead mode with hatred, convinced that everything connected with it was evil, and believing
that what was the opposite to it, what was its coun-
terpart, must be good. This means the beginning
of a philosophy, and of that particular species
which expresses itself as a philosophy of two
worlds.

THE PHILOSOPHY OF TWO WORLDS. In the time of
Dante there were in Florence two political parties
known as the *Neri* and the *Bianci*. Lawrence has
many connections with Tuscany: he might have
named his worlds after these two factions.

Neri and Bianci. Blacks and Whites. Dark and
Light.

It is an old way to divide the universe. Body and
spirit. Below and above.

In the *Phædrus* Plato speaks of the two halves as
a team of two horses driven by a charioteer:

'The right-hand horse is upright and cleanly
made, and has a lofty neck and an aquiline nose:
his colour is white . . . he is a lover of honesty
and modesty and temperance, and the follower of
true glory. . . .

'Whereas the other is a crooked animal . . . he
is flat faced and of a dark colour. . . .'

The same two worlds, but the difference lies in
which way the sympathy goes. Real philosophers
are less than anybody 'philosophical' in the sense
of being urbanely detached from what they write

about. There is never any doubt in Plato which of the two horses he cares less for.

Socrates, Pythagoras or whoever it was in Greece or Arabia whose image for the life growing in himself was the image of spirit rising upwards out of the body created such a vivid metaphor that though it has been adopted by Christianity and every idealist ethic, virtue has scarcely yet gone out of it. Even now thought seems impossible without its terminology. Sublime: lofty: exalted: enlightenment: climbing ever higher: *higher mammals: higher education*. Yet to Lawrence this imagery is the language of everything in the world he most hates.

He reverses it, therefore. *Dark* comes in instead. Dark, dark, *endarkenment* he would say. His readers know he does not hide his dark under a bushel. He reverses Plato.

The novelty of this reversed idealism, and the fact that Lawrence propounds it in most of his books has its advantages. The definiteness of this surface moral makes his writing in some way palatable. His method of stating every question in terms of the opposition of two contraries has force. Science discussion, the motive of life, leadership of men, cosmogonies are all expressed antithetically. Lamb – Tiger. Love – Power. Sympathetic ganglia – repelling ganglia. Mankind – individuals.

But two-world philosophers want you to hate one of their worlds and desire the other. If they are novelists, therefore, they have heroes and villains and heavens and hells; and hero-villain novels are

always at their weakest when a 'hero-villain' atmosphere predominates. It is wrong to think that not
to take sides is god-like, unless taking sides means
being permanently one-sided. There is just this
wrong sort of permanence about heroes and villains.

THE LAWRENCE HERO. By the hero I do not mean the
small dark person who is the protagonist of many of
the novels – *Women in Love*, for instance. Him I
will call the Lawrence man. The Lawrence heroes,
or the permanent side of them, represent Lawrence's
ideal man. The type is Aaron Sisson, in *Aaron's
Rod*. As near as possible he is the reverse of Hamlet. Neither introspective, self-hating, incapable of
translating thought into action, nor intellectual. On
the contrary, deep though his feelings are, he cannot speak them except in so far as the imposed
necessities of a novel awkwardly insist. The surface
complications which prevent Hamlet from behaving
in accordance with his real wants are absent, the
most important result of which is that in the issue
which Lawrence makes the chief test – namely the
sex issue – he is never at a loss. He never 'uses'
sex for pleasure or childbearing; nor does he suffer
Hamlet's revulsions. Continence and incontinence
– neither words have any connection with him,
since all his relationships rise not from predetermina-
tions but from inner impulse. Therefore in his
sexual relationships particularly, successful experience will be eventually certain.

It is an attempt to express positively what Shake-speare is expressing negatively, the necessity for allowing the real self to act without being thwarted by a wilful ego. The complete bodily health of the Lawrence hero follows as automatically as his complete shamelessness.

Lawrence holds up his hero before us, but stresses the fact that his hero doesn't hold *himself* up as an ideal, or try to alter people to suit him, or exert his will – his 'superficial' will or determina-tion – to alter other people and himself. But neither will he allow other people to alter him. If he does flag, this steed in Lawrence's team only needs direct relationship with the impulse im-parted by the charioteer (a relation he does not avoid) to be perfectly fulfilled.

The Lawrence heroine, who is, like the hero, largely and luxuriously formed, is related to him in other ways except in the important respect that she is inclined to fall back, in the deepest issues, on the certainty of the charioteer behind her. She has a womanly lack of infallibility; it is always a question, as with Kate in *The Plumed Serpent*, of overcoming a *slight* unwillingness to abandon her-self. She is always a *little* more influenced by the handicaps and consciousness of modern life. She cannot stand entirely alone, or she casts too many regretful glances back towards the things she only thinks she wants. Nevertheless she will in the end be as completely fulfilled – by means, particularly, of sexual experience. For, as with the hero, she is fortunate, and heroic, in never being in the position of Lover Loving Not Loved.

HEAVEN AND HELL. The Lawrence heaven is a world away from 'factories, jazz and cinemas' chiefly. It is placed preferably in the luxuriant semi-tropical parts of the earth where the sun and moon are brilliant. Where the towns are small, unmodern, and not too clean. Where the inhabitants are members of a dark-coloured aboriginal race not too buttoned up in conventional clothing. A mixture of brilliant sun, bodies, desert places, and intense dark.

Then there is the reverse hell, the Satan of which is fair and civilised. Oxford-cultured; uneasy; often literary in a careful way. No dignity. No central quietness. He either deliberately over-indulges in sex by way of 'seeing life,' or he is symbolically impotent. The villainess is full of romantic fancies, or else arch-villainously practical minded. She either forms intimacies with men and withdraws from sexual contact when that is offered with a bridling 'none of that,' or she is a female ravisher. These qualities are not to be explained pathologically, but on the contrary the key to the frequent illnesses and deaths of these people lies strictly in their character, in their egoistic thwarting of self. It is a reversal of psycho-analytic doctrine.

The hell itself is the mechanical world – that part

of this world which is lived under imposed ideals.
One also gets the impression that this hell is peculiar in having a temperate climate, where the
sunlight and moonlight are proportionately thin,
the towns with their roads clean, their weekly
papers entertaining, their Bohemian sets perky: the
countryside so hedged over and railed round as to
be neither one thing nor the other. Everything is
worn thin. In the provinces, idealism worn thin:
in the towns, the intellectual artiness and nothing-
shock-us attitude worn thin. A world where everything is experienced exclusively in the head and
talked to pieces there — above all sex, continually,
talked scientifically, talked humorously, talked sen-
sibly, talked tolerantly. 'Sex in the head.' The hell
is on the whole remarkably like England, not least
in the fact that its inhabitants, the white and villain-
ous horses of Lawrence's team, wilfully refuse to
abandon themselves to the wishes of their leader.

'THE LAWRENCE MAN.' Besides the team, there is
the charioteer as well — either in the books or only
just outside them. The charioteer — the man between the two worlds — is the 'Lawrence man.'
Birkin, in *Women in Love*: Lilley, in *Aaron's Rod*:
Somers, in *Kangaroo*. He is small and sensitive,
quiet and contained, distant and attractive. He can
cook his own meals, and tell the names of the
colours and materials of women's clothes. He is
familiar with trees and flowers and shells. He

shows the good quality of the dark heaven in ability to abandon himself to experience and the enacting of his wants; and borrows from the hell of enlightenment the gift of being able to give his feelings intellectual expression. He is a kind of leader, and dark heroes follow him: he is a kind of butt, and is despised and rejected by the light villains.

THE DARK GOD. There is only one gap to fill, what for Plato's charioteer was The Idea. Lawrence at first leaves this unnamed – till he begins to call it the thing *between* the two worlds, the infinite between the two absolutes. Later he begins to call it 'god,' and finally it is definite as the Dark God. Giving it a name everything is accounted for. The philosophy is complete.

THE PHILOSOPHY SUMMED UP.
'And is this all there is in him?'

Emphatically not, but it is a fair summary of his gist.

'Then surely we should not be missing anything if we never read a line of him? There is nothing new about it – a mere anti-intellectual philosophy, or boosting of the unconscious. His hatred of ideas – "like nails stuck into the bark of a growing tree" – it is all put much more fully by Schopenhauer in illustration of the proposition that ideas are only

substitutes — the feeble echo of a full response to a
stimulus of which we are no longer capable. Isn't
he one of the reason haters Socrates used to make
fun of, calling them misologists? And his cracking
up of dark races. We know all about the Noble
Savage. Of course he is only an intellectual himself,
because of course all intellectuals, from Kant
onwards, belittle the intellect. And the emphasis
he lays on the acceptance of the body — isn't it all
more explicit in Nietzsche and more magnificent in
Whitman? And we don't want to be told at length
that Christian values are worn out. That was said
more constructively in a certain six pages by
William Blake. Nor are we dependent on *The
Plumed Serpent* for the record of an attempt to
give meaning to the concept of God in terms of
modern experience, since we already have Middleton
Murry's absorbing record of such an attempt,
certainly not less sincere because of its acceptance
of Christ. And isn't it also true to say that most of
these opinions about life have been demonstrated
in books and lectures for ten years over two con-
tinents by Count Hermann Keyserling, uniformity
with whose views and ways of speaking might not
always be considered valid recommendation?'

It is true that if there was nothing in Lawrence
but consistent theory, even if this were overwhelmingly novel, it would be unnecessary to read him.
It would be still more unnecessary to write about
him, because the conclusions drawn would be
nothing more than mere agreement or disagreement

with conclusions which had themselves arisen in the same way.

If, on the other hand, there is to be found in Lawrence's work a new world and a new person, the case is altered. Then instead of the philosophy being the clue to Lawrence, it will be Lawrence who is the clue to the philosophy, which will itself become an important part of the general meaning of his whole work.

PART TWO
AUTOBIOGRAPHY

AUTOBIOGRAPHY

Is it possible to study Lawrence himself? Writers are rarely accessible – even 'autobiographical' ones.

It is well known that Lawrence is an autobiographical writer in one sense, that he is always 'putting people into books.' He has occasionally made public unforgivable secrets, and he would consider it unforgivable to hesitate to do so for reasons of kindness or even gratitude. He does not, that is to say, spare feelings. But that fact in itself is scarcely sufficient to ensure truth.

The vast majority of writers – English writers especially – are most retiring when they set out to be most revealing. Charles Lamb is the type. There is a sense in which he always writes about 'I,' and a sense in which he never does. We know nothing of *him*, though we know his character – the character of the whimsical, badly dressed, humorous, tragic small man up to which he always lived so rigidly and which he explains so humorously. It is a paradox, but it is necessary to get to know writers in order to collect evidence of the possibility of knowing them.

'The sounding cataract Haunted me like a passion' sounds almost like good steady journalism. What diction! But the author is Wordsworth in his twenties, therefore we know it is revelation. Wordsworth is autobiographical in that passage.

Yet can even men like Wordsworth claim the

word 'autobiographical' for their work? Is the
Prelude, besides being a record of living moments,
a record of growth also — as Zarathustra is a record
of growth? In this chapter there must be an
attempt to make this difference between what
represents Lawrence's real development or at any
rate the real 'moments,' on the one hand, and the
self-portraiture, descriptions of character, and human
passages common to all writers on the other.
Nothing essential will be based on fact of biogra-
phical detail. This study of development is founded
almost entirely on the sequence of the books
themselves.

§1. THE FAILURE OF LOVE

['The White Peacock'; 'The Trespasser'; 'Sons and
Lovers'; 'Early Poems']

[*Note.* Actual quotations from Lawrence are in this autobiographical section (i.e. up to page 92) indicated exclusively by
italics.]

'THAT I love my mother better than my father.'

Then: 'That my mother is better than my father.'

Then: 'That my mother is superior to my father
in what she knows about; superior in what she reads
and speaks of. She is small and neat; he is loutish.

'My mother is something to be imitated. Her
more delicate speech and accent, her tidiness, her
superior knowledge. My father is something not
to be imitated.'

*His manner got worse and worse, his habits somewhat
disgusting. When the children were growing up and
in the crucial stage of adolescence, the father was like
some ugly irritant to their souls.* All the miners in all
the houses down the row were just the same. Each
one coming in half drunk, and still unwashed, from
the mine. Bad surroundings, Lawrence thought,
for a young poet.

He must get clear from this. He knew he could,
in spite of this unlucky start. At the same time
there was the extraordinary love between his mother
and himself. With this how confidently could be
surmounted the earthiness of his surroundings.

'For *I know* I am going to be something. I am
so often overwhelmed — by these extraordinary
feelings. Take my friendship with the young
farmer, with George. There is nothing ordinary
about it, it completely envelopes everything. Moreover he recognises something in me too — and of
course so does my mother. Then how curious it is
when she is ill — how overwhelmed and "floored" I
am by that. Also there is the way I notice things;
the wonderful pleasure I get from noticing ordinary
objects — gorse-bushes, peewits — the thousands of
rabbits that ruin over the farmland belonging to
Miriam's house — *handfulls of brown earth* in my
poem. I am a poet. My extraordinary spring
feelings.

'*How splendid it is to be substance, here!* I "stand
tiptoe." When I go out with George and his gun
in the evening, I see these things.

'Yet I don't speak of them to him: I keep them
more to myself. If I do speak it is to my other
friend, to Miriam, who is more my intellectual
equal: she understands my ideas perfectly, better
even than my mother. She also, like me, seems
burning with the intensity of her feelings: she is
not prim and logical; she understands me better.
She belongs more to my poetical world.'

*Everything had a religious and intensified meaning
when he was with her*. She appreciated beauty —
the celandines: as she said how could anyone want
streets paved with gold when there are these yellow
flowers? George would never have made this fine

D . H . LAWRENCE *aged 21*

In answer to a question, Lawrence wrote of the existence of this portrait which showed him, he said, as a " clean shaven, bright young prig in a high collar like a curate, guaranteed to counteract all the dark and sinister effect of all the newspaper photographs."

comment. She must be the right person for him. How unlike the foul mines, and his father's ordinariness. *The girl was romantic in her soul. Everywhere was a Walter Scott heroine being loved by men with helmets or with plumes in their caps . . . she was afraid lest this boy, who nevertheless looked something like a Walter Scott hero, who could paint and speak French, might consider her simply as the swine-girl, unable to perceive the princess beneath.*

She need not have been afraid — the wonderful thoughts they had, standing together before a burning sunset. Feelings of reverence — the presence of God — the sky becoming dark like a cathedral. Her intensity: in a sense it seemed to correspond to something in him.

Later on, when they grew older, they made daring assaults together on accepted things. They would help to do something to make poverty come to an end: they would learn about social conditions, and help their fellow-men. They were suddenly overwhelmed by the realisation of what seemed to them a degraded world: they felt so far above everything — the rest of the world they suddenly saw *as a pool from which the waters are drained off, leaving the water things to wrestle in the wet mud under the sun.* Then they would attack religion — its doctrine part. Or at least they read Renan's *Vie de Jésus.* He began to move away from his mother now. Quite right — he must not be held back. 'Woman, what have I to do with thee?' He could see she hated Miriam, and was jealous of her.

They read more and more modern books together. It was extraordinary the way Miriam seemed to 'sympathise' with what he wanted, although Miriam hated his agnosticism: but it was too religious an agnosticism for her to suffer badly.

You woke my spirit, you bore me to consciousness — for a time he could scarcely have lived without her.

Meanwhile Lawrence was twenty-one, and there was something else awakening in him of a different nature. He was virgin.

> *Now and again*
> *The life that looks through my eyes*
> *And behaves like the rest of men*
> *Slips away, so I gasp in surprise.*
> *. . . Then willy-nilly*
> *A lower me gets up and greets me*
> *Homunculus stirs from his roots. . . .*
> *Dark, ruddy pillar, forgive me! I*
> *Am helplessly bound*
> *To the rock of virginity.*
> > *Thy tower impinges*
> *On nothingness. Pardon me!*[1]

Now came a crisis. The change in Lawrence was insistent. Could Miriam share new experience with him? Presumably. She was a woman, and moreover equally ready to go daringly ahead with him — free and emancipated; so he approached her. Yes, of

[1] The early poem *Virgin Youth*, as rewritten 1928.

course, as he thought, she saw nothing wrong in it, or not when he had talked to her. '*You don't think it ugly?*' he asked. '*No, not now. You have taught me it isn't.*' She would have connection with him. The experience was coming of which he had read and heard so much. Poets write of it. It would be certain to change him completely. *The test was on Miriam.* Could she go this step farther with him?

Lawrence was disappointed. They lay together, but where was the overwhelming change that he expected? Why did he not at once begin to be a much more expressive man, much more of a great man than before? He continued to see her as often as ever, but now there was an atmosphere of failure about their relationship. He could not yet say what it was. Soon he was sure of this: that there were beginning to be things in Miriam which he felt were wrong, characteristics which he could not bear. Was it her *intensity?* Her hands, he noted, were never allowed to hang down loosely by her side, half opened. They were stiff. He did not like either the way she 'adored' over her baby brother, bending down over him in a sort of agony; it made him uncomfortable. Her way of being religious — he didn't like that either. 'I believe you are more religious when you don't have occasion to be worrying and thinking about it' — he became sure of this.

One evening they are lying together out of doors,

and he sees Miriam's face in a flash of summer lightning. It seems to him that she is afraid of him, and afraid of what she is doing: she is not *lost* in his arms, she is doing it all for his sake: he sees in her face almost resignation, as if she was a sacrifice.

Now Lawrence began to hate his relationship with Miriam. The flash of lightning had made something clear to him. He didn't know cause nor reason for it: but

> *Almost I hated her, sacrificed;*
> *Hated myself, and the place. . . .*

It was a terrible set-back. Instead of 'finding' himself as he had hoped through this experience, he was only unsettled. He became full of self-dislike. He began to turn against everything he had grown up with.

Therefore he did what he was often to do afterwards. He left the scene of his dislikes and revulsions in the hope of leaving his revulsions behind too.

He went to earn his living in London, to teach in a school. The day of Miriam was over.

'Now I must get on with bringing out what I know is in me — let my powers have room to develop.' Like other young men, he found the town 'barren,' and the outskirts 'dreary.' He was in that part of the suburbs where the Crystal Palace makes sudden and gigantic appearances between house-rows. He longed for the Nottingham country again, but he was able to write poems expressing the longing. He was started.

As a teacher he had meant not to follow the run of schoolmasters but to treat the boys naturally, and talk to them as human beings of curiously differing individuality. He found this an unaccountable failure. On the other hand he was successful in being able to begin his first book, his first novel.

He believed he had been successful at last, too, in meeting the woman he longed to find: *really* emancipated and really free, in the way he was. An intellectual equal, but no denier of the body like Miriam – a delightful and fascinating woman. He writes poems in which she is called 'Helena.' He goes right away from London with her in the August holiday to the English sea-coast. It seems perfect – she certainly has no thought of wrong-doing, or of anything being ugly. . . .

But after the fortnight alone with her – again he feels a terrible disappointment. Where is the re-incarnated, the new-made man he expects himself to be? He still feels unsatisfied; he knows that it is by means of a woman that he is to grow, yet so far there has been no real change in him. True there is his novel. *The White Peacock* – there is something there it is certain. Something begins to emerge; Cyril is a definite person; but isn't it largely himself as he was at Nottingham in the Miriam days? As he reads it over, don't some of the sentences sound desperately like the young-intellectual talk he feels he should have left behind now? Talk about *life, sex, and its origins; of Schopenhauer and William James.*

And think of this sentence:

You are like Burne-Jones damsels. Troublesome shadows are always crowding across your eyes, and you cherish them. You think the flesh of the apple is nothing, nothing. You only care for the eternal pips.

Talking about eternal pips when it was high time he was recording vivid passionate experiences. The only relationship passionately recorded in the book is the one between himself and his friend: between Cyril and George, *friendship at its mystical best,* and even the sincerity of that does not always come through the language.

While Lawrence was seeking himself in London, the experience he wanted came from the home he was trying to break clear of. He had already partly realised that the connection between himself and his mother was more powerful than any other in his life. The completeness of the pleasure sometimes, even if he was only walking by her side, was like nothing else he felt. Now the equal completeness of the pain in his own body because she was suffering in hers made the connection seem ten times stronger. His mother was dying of a hopeless and terrible disease. He began to suffer in a new way, and to change.

While his mother was very ill he went often to see her. He came back to Nottingham for a time.

Whatever she said to him at this period he remembered. He understood why she had never approved of Miriam, '*and I've never — you know, Paul — I've never had a husband — not really.*' He began at this time to realise how much more vivid and absorbing his contact with his mother had been — how extended beyond the average passionate feeling of a little boy — how far more important than Miriam or Helen.

As his mother became worse he seemed all pain and nothing else — no thoughts of what he was going to do, how he was getting on, whether Helen was helping him or not. He was in some way simplified by his pain. His mother, in her despair, told him things which gave him agony — how she had hated her husband and been unhappy. Lawrence suffered overwhelmingly: still, he found he was able to suffer. Though so far his writing only gave a hint of it, there was something inside him to meet and feel the wave: he was not swept away. He was struck down — his way of life, even the directions of his ambition were broken: yet still the beginning of him remained.

For a time he was inert, feeling himself like a gap in his surroundings. What a place to be melancholy in, the south parts of London, when in autumn the gardens beneath the London chestnuts and limes became marshy with cold leaves and autumn wet. Lawrence stares at the window, *watching for night to waft a meaning or a message over the window glass.*

As he stares the sense of freedom which extreme sorrow gives impresses on him. He begins to know things which he did not know before. He begins to know that his mother in some way held him back —

> *My little love, my dearest,*
> *Twice you have issued me,*
> *Once from your womb, sweet mother,*
> *Once from your soul, to be*
> *Free of all hearts, my darling,*
> *Of each heart's entrance free.*

It was some time before this sorrow sank through Lawrence. When it had left him, the change which he hoped for had come about. He knew more deeply and his knowledge became definite. He was made expressive. He knew how fundamental the connection had been between his mother and himself. He would write a book as the result of experience through a woman after all, but it would be his mother — the most important woman in it would have to be his mother. Knowing this, he believed he understood all his past dissatisfactions and past failures. Why he had left Nottingham. What he had been suffering from. What had been wrong with Miriam, with his parents, with the school and his teaching, with Helena. Why the death of his mother should give him this knowledge he did not know; but the change brought about in him seemed to disentangle him from his teens and his

Nottingham days, and make him *see* what it was he had hated. He could now give a name to it.

He could see it as a worn-out way of living. He called it the worn-out Christian love-ideal. In *Sons and Lovers* he recorded how always, he thought, he must have disliked it. The way Christian resignation was over everything, the way Miriam's family, for instance, lived even the trivial parts of their lives in terms of it. *The mother exalted everything — even a bit of housework — to the plane of a religious trust. The sons resented this; they felt themselves cut away underneath . . . it puzzled Paul*: of course it was what was wrong with Miriam. He seemed to have known it always: *this 'purity' which prevented even their first love kiss.* Oh, he was glad he was rid of Miriam. *Love should give a sense of freedom, not of prison. Miriam made me feel tied up like a donkey to a stake. I must feed on her patch and nowhere else.*

When he first came to London he had not been clear of it, he now knew. Trying to teach the boys in his classes by love, getting at them through love — it was indecent and stupid. I shall not do it again. *I shall keep my strength for myself.* It was the controlling character of this sort of love — the bullying, the intellectual bullying which he most disliked.

It all went, he thought, with *ideas*; having ideas of things, of behaviour, of sex also. As with Miriam, so with Helen, having ideas of what love should be, and in the case of Helen wanting to know everything — in the head. Helen saw life through what she read. To her *the rippling sunlight on the sea was the Rhine maidens spreading their light hair to the sun* . . . not so to Lawrence. If only he could stop her insistent dreaming and worried thinking which was keeping back her real passion.

> *Close your eyes, my love, let me make you blind*
> > *They have taught you to see*
> *Only problems writ on the face of things,*
> *And algebra in the eyes of desirous men.*

But it was useless. She didn't love him, she loved the romance of loving him.

> *And now I know, so I must be ashamed;*
> *You love me while I hover tenderly*
> *Like moonbeams kissing you.*

This was the end of intellectualism and idealism for Lawrence. It was the end of the 'love-mode.' There was one thing Lawrence felt sure that he now wanted — to be left alone and allowed to develop the shoots of life that were rising in him. Love was the thing which would never leave you alone. Even his mother had dragged at him with her love.

> *Love is the great asker*
> *The sun and rain do not ask the secret*
> *Of the time when the grain struggles down in the dark*
> *. . . ever at my side,*
> *Frail and sad, with grey, bowed head.*
> *The beggar-woman, the yearning eyed*
> *Inexorable love goes lagging.*

Love was a failure – Lawrence believed he was certain of it. Love for him meant now controlling love, itself the result of a command: 'Love one another.' Now he would leave it all – the emancipated English women, the English moon, people who 'win souls,' women ill at ease to know. It seemed that for him there was no room for development in that world.

Well, he said good-bye to it, and with only one single touch of doubt, looking at Helen, and her coolness, and her clear and delicate spirit. He was to leave this for ever. . . . He must not have such regrets and backward glances. He felt new things beginning in him.

D

§2. THE FIRST STEP TO FULFILMENT

['Look! We Have Come Through!'; 'The Rainbow']

I am myself at last; now I achieve
My very self . . . perfected from my fellow.

In spite of his failure with Miriam and Helena Lawrence was convinced that it was through sex experience the new Lawrence would come. The Christian love-idealists were such deniers of the body; it seemed self-evident this must be his way of fulfilment. Since his mother's death, too, he had become more certain; for before there had been another woman, a third woman, superficially prude-like, but really with deep voluptuous reserves and power of abandonment. That he should have failed, as he did, equally with her made him feel at the time almost like an impotent man.

However, since his mother's death, his sense of the coming power to experience had become conviction. The wave was mounting inside him. It did not matter that he had found Miriam came short — or was it *himself*? Was the insufficiency in himself? Perhaps he should have been able to bear down all their tentativeness by his positive conviction. He was sure he could now.

Therefore Lawrence did meet the woman he wanted.

His first writings, the first words of the new Lawrence, are poems composed over a period of three years. In these there is no clear record.

There are different kinds of struggles. The woman is already married, and already has children whom she cannot always cut free from, even when she is separated from them by countries. There is also the struggle of the wish, put down in brief poems, to melt away the ego barrier, the hard personality part which is a fence between each of them. This is achieved: Lawrence's great wish is granted: the mounting wave in him bursts in action.

> *Not I, not I, but the wind that blows through me,*
> *A fine wind is blowing the new direction of Time*
> *If only I let it bear me, carry me, if only it carry me.*

It is with some such feeling of new power that he writes *The Rainbow*. It is full of a certain positive quality, warmth, and *naïveté*. A quiet unsophistication — Lawrence will praise the earth and life connected with it as against the life of the intellect — romantic but sincere. The people in the book are farmers and farmers' sons who *knew the intercourse between heaven and earth, sunshine drawn into the breast and bowels*. Milking, *the pulse of the blood of the teats of the cows beat into the pulse of the hands of the men*. Lawrence is an unskilful, but a warm and fulfilled man in this novel. There are accounts of marriages and the life of lovers idealised and 'beautified.' *She did not know him only she knew he was a man come for her*. He can judge, now, the relations between men and women in terms of what had happened to him and of what he now knows is possible. The marriage of Anna and Will, for instance, becomes a failure; there is strife between them, until something makes Will stop his desire to *alter*, to bully Anna at a distance, after which there is relaxation and fulfilment, so far as their limitations will allow.

Lawrence is able to record this as part of his new experience. It is the result of the new man he has become. One of the things he can say he knows is that union is the wrong word for perfect meeting in marriage. He often returns to this in poems. It is not a mingling, but a mutual exchange of revelation. This enriches, but makes isolation more complete, because increase of experience reduces the extent of that unrealised part of the world, which, in the form of preconception, we possess in common with other people.

> *And yet all the while you are you, you are not me*
> *And I am I, I am never you*
> *. . . Yet I am glad you are something I shall*
> *never be . . .*
> *I shall never cease to be filled with newness*
> *Having you near me.*

In *The Rainbow* Lawrence can not yet give an account of this absolute meeting between man and woman: he does not know it well enough. But his new estate has given him a new criterion of people, and this he does make use of, and apply. He writes of the men and women in *The Rainbow* as possessed or not possessed of the powers of contact. He writes of them as possessed or not possessed of a certain 'centrality' -- a self beneath the ego.

In *The White Peacock* there was something like the same distinction implied. There was George, who, drinking himself to death because of his failure to take Lettie, allowed his real self to be killed away by his character, a tragedy of character, the positive wants of the self destroyed by the 'negative passions' of the character. Then, contrasted with George, Lawrence makes felt the force of Cyril, in whom was everything George lacked.

Quite different, however, in *The Rainbow*. All the characters are shown in clear terms of this definite distinction — their possession or lack of this essential which Lawrence now knows to be in himself.

There is one person in *The Rainbow* who has it completely — Ursula: one who has it not at all — her lover Skrebensky. Here the difference is brought out dramatically, in Ursula's leaving Skrebensky, and being obedient to herself rather than to her feelings of pity: in Skrebensky's horror and collapse, when he is thrust back on a self which is not there. He is possessed by the *horror of not-being*. He becomes only *a cold surface of consciousness*. He can *have no experiences of any sort*. As Ursula says of him: *It's all such a nothingness, what he feels and what he doesn't feel*. Disloyal to him, Ursula is loyal to her own centrality. Afterwards she regrets, repents, and is ill and miserable. But all the time

she had a dull firmness of being, a sense of permanency.
Lawrence himself – he feels this, he feels he is
about to sweep onwards. He has achieved real
growth, and it is to be the prelude to more. Nothing
will stop him now. If he had a wish, it would be
that he could be sure that his own 'Ursula's' new
knowledge was co-equal with his own, that he could
be sure that she also had gained, through their
new experience, a new knowledge of the absolute
difference between them. *She has not realised yet,
the fearful thing, that I am the other.* But nevertheless, knowing his own centre, he knows his own
future. The metaphor of *The Rainbow* – naïve but
fitting; or the metaphor of spring.

> *The gush of spring is strong enough*
> *To play with the globe of earth like a ball on a*
>   *fountain;*
> *At the same time it opens the tiny hands of the*
>   *hazel*
> *With such infinite patience. . . .*
> *Ah come, come quickly, spring!*
> *Come and lift us towards our culmination, we*
>   *myriads:*
> *We who have never flowered, like patient*
>   *cactuses.*

Nothing can stop me now, not I myself.

> *Not I, not I, but the wind that blows through me,*
> *A fine wind is blowing the new direction of Time.*

§3. THE IMPEDIMENT

['The Crown'; 'Women in Love'; 'Fantasia of the Unconscious']

No sooner had Lawrence made the succesful start than he encountered an impediment in his way.

If only I let it bear me, carry me, if only I let it carry me.

This was Lawrence's prayer, arising from the vision of the possibilities of living which was made plain to him after this one period. But his prayer was not answered.

The reason, it must have seemed to Lawrence, was the accident of his position in time and space: the fact that he was a young man in England at the time of the war.

At first he seemed stimulated by it. He wrote a long essay[1] for a small magazine started by Middleton Murry. It was very good; half-formulated thoughts seemed to have been given shape by the suggestive text of the fact of the war. He was able to put better his attitude to idealism. He expresses his opposition to the way of life he hated with vividness. More important than this essay, the novel, which was to be the new action resulting from the bringing to consciousness of his new experiences, began to take shape.[2] There was no mention of the war in it, but, like the essay, his

[1] *The Crown.*   [2] *Women in Love.*

writing had taken on a new, strong, definite quality; things which were only implied in *Look We Have Come Through* are made explicit here. The way of life he is breaking from is described dramatically in relationships between characters in the book. Many issues are made clear. A giant enemy, a Goliath, is placed in the forefront: a hero is opposed. It is a war book.

This, however, was all before Lawrence himself was affected. For he was affected by the war in this way, that part of him came near to being ruined — was perhaps finally ruined by it.

As the war went on, Lawrence began to find himself surrounded by men taking definable attitudes. Either, it seemed, they fought on principle or else they did not fight on principle; and then there were others who because they were unprincipled avoided militarism on the one hand or pacificism on the other for reasons of personal comfort. All these attitudes were definite and easy to follow and so met the public need. But there was another section still, and of these Lawrence felt himself to be one, whose feelings were equally definite but far more difficult to put clearly: men who did not belong to, or at any rate were trying to break away from, the whole world to which idealism and principles and wars on behalf of them belonged. How could Lawrence say 'I don't want to fight because really I am utterly disconnected from all this.' Or: 'I agree that I am under a moral obligation to help in the defence of the country when I share in its advantages, but I am not acting on moral grounds — quite the contrary — in fact that is the whole point. You see I am trying to do what I *want*.' Lawrence found that such words became impertinent abstractions to everyone but himself. It was useless even to speak them. He had to be silent.

He did not write about the actual details till years after it happened. There is a chapter in *Kangaroo*, 'The Nightmare,' which gives bare facts. Even after the interval he cannot speak about it without blinding indignation. It was ignominious even to have to think of the experience of a conscientious objector who was not conscientious, who was mixed up with conscription, but who for reasons of health was never actually conscripted. The periodical medical examination. Wretched medical orderlies telling him to bend down and touch his toes while they looked him over as if he were cattle. *Cochons!* And then just because he was short and had a beard and looked like a foreigner, or because his wife was a naturalised German, when he tried to escape to a cottage in Cornwall *spies* would lie outside the window of his room and make notes of what he said.

He could not blame them, they scarcely knew what they were doing. The village people sometimes refused to speak to them in the streets.

It was not this he minded so much. The terrible thing was that he should be vulnerable, that he should be *touched* by this. Yet he believed they could see, in spite of everything, that he was different. His indignation at the unreasonable suspicion under which he and his wife lived came to a head when one evening they came back to their cottage to find every room had been searched and every drawer turned inside out. The officer in charge of the business had come to the house, and Lawrence had looked him over, just looked at him, without answering what he said. . . . *To him they were not: they were just things, obeying orders, and his eyes showed that. The young officer wanted to get out.* Puppies. But they must see what he felt about them.

Lawrence, who was going to be the new man, who was going to live on his own, in the great sense, had come to this. To pitting his dignity against schoolboy officers.

He had always believed so in everything — society, love, friends.

He wrote nothing but a few poems; poorly expressive. It seemed useless even to try. His novel, *The Rainbow*, which he was certain was better than anything he had written before, had been banned from publication as indecent. A serious famous playwright had given him dignified advice.[1]

---

[1] Lawrence writes bitterly about the banning of *The Rainbow* in his foreword to E. D. MacDonald's bibliography: 'Methuen published the book, and he almost wept before the magistrate, when he was summoned for bringing out a piece of indecent literature. . . . In print my fellow-authors kept scrupulously silent, lest a bit of tar might stick to them. Later Arnold Bennett and May Sinclair raised a kindly protest. But John Galsworthy . . . impromptu opinions by elderly authors . . . There is no more indecency or impropriety in *The Rainbow* than there is in this autumn morning.'

Nobody had noticed the *Crown* essay. *Women in Love* he would keep in manuscript.

> *the soul is still compressed;*
> *I carry my patience sullenly through the waste lands.*

He who had determined never to be intellectually bullied, but to live independently of the world where such a thing was possible! Intellectual bullying — that was the very thing which in *The Rainbow* he had shown to be the great enemy — in a sense the only enemy — of life. Yet now he is soiled and neutralised by this very thing. They are trying to force him into something he is not. But he will not be downed by it. He will wait, and swear inwardly that then, when it is all over, he will free himself, get rid of it for ever, and make it impossible for it ever to happen again.

* * * *

> *Have we had an innings?*
> *God forfend.*

It would seem that the blank the war put on him was only temporary. At any rate no sooner was peace made than his silence changed to fertility. For ten years long novels, large books of essays and short stories, poems and pamphlets issue steadily from Secker's offices. They are square-looking brown books, full of pages, and the pages very full of print. He seems certainly to have changed also or his way of writing has altered as it altered in the

first years of the war. He writes like a man who
has made up his mind. He writes at passionate
length, all the unwritten stuff inside him, hibernated
during the war, comes coiling out of him. He wants
to account for everything that has happened.

First of all must be said what in a sense certainly
he has said before. He wants to say it now with far
greater vigour and conviction — that of course the
whole war, the whole thing was the result of exactly
that bad factor which he had managed to isolate out
of modern life; the worn-out mode, idealism. True,
he had already thought it out and written it down in
the early days of the war, and true again that *there
was always confusion in speech. Yet it must be spoken.*

Further, also, there was the actual practical
necessity for speaking which had been made alarm-
ingly clear during the war: the fact that if he did
not make it clear what was happening to the world,
he might suffer again. He could never survive
being damaged a second time. When he writes
now, there is no writing 'for the few' about it. *If I
could but advise, I would advise that this notice should
be sent through the length and breadth of the land.* It
is not a question of 'he that hath ears.' Everyone
must hear: if they do they must understand: it is
necessary for my survival. Lawrence had never seen
so clearly; neither had he known so distinctly the
necessity of writing.

Within two years he had published *Women in
Love.*[1] If it was for want of being understood that

[1] First printed privately in America, November 1920.

he was not read before the war, he would not let
that be a reason now. *Women in Love* should be
placed at the forefront of his work. In it there would
be found no passage unexplained: and everything in
his world would be covered. Every chapter had its
own special point, and represented something which
Lawrence, with his new powers, had been able to
clear up. In the beginning is a character: not a
person, a character, new to literature, placed terribly
in the front of the book, and overshadowing it. It
is hardly even a character so much as a denuncia-
tion – Lawrence has been longing to write it – of
the *bully* he has suffered from. All the people who
have tried to get at him, to alter him into an approxi-
mation of themselves, are denounced in Hermione
Roddice. Not physical bullying, or intellectual
bullying, but bullying of his own integrity. If only
I can *put her down*, he says of Hermione.

Just as physical bullying is a sign of lack of physical fulfilment, so integrity bullying must be a sign
of lack of self. Hermione's activity is partly this,
and partly an attempt to force an acknowledgment of
herself – of somebody, that is, who she cannot bear
to realise has no real existence.

Lawrence makes her the opposite of himself. So
far from wanting contact with people *she seeks to
make herself invulnerable, beyond reach of the world's
judgment*. But there was a flaw in her armour. *It
was a lack of robust self; she had no natural sufficiency,
there was a terrible lack, a deficiency of being within
her*. However much she might build up intellectual

outworks of sensibility to the arts and knowledge of artistic subjects and movements and dogmas of living 'beautifully,' perhaps helpfully – sometimes almost forcing other people to live 'beautifully' too – she could not avoid the truth.

Lawrence sets up this fearful Goliath, this symbol, at the beginning of the book. So far as the way his antagonism goes, it is as before the war. But now there is a great change, a champion, a David, a 'Lawrence man': the Lawrence man appears, to attack the Goliaths. 'I will put her down.' Lawrence *versus* the world where such people can exist.

Before the rest of the novel can be written, Birkin has to knock down Hermione. Actually, in the novel, Hermione knocks down Birkin. In a madness of frustrated sexual passion, she knocks Birkin on the head with a lapis-lazuli ornament; but he wriggles clear; he gets out, and does for her – like David, at a distance – by the negative method of not being affected by her, not giving in to her, not being what she wants him to be. He keeps clear.

This part of the book written, there is a sense of pressure relieved. Having got rid of the evil, Lawrence is free to turn to its causes. He now sees them so clearly. Explanations come to his mind with more attendant analogies and examples than ever before. It is all owing to something wrong in our activities – that is the essential. So its result in life cannot better be explained than by a word which, for some reason, implies activity of a wrong sort – namely corruption.

He can see exactly how the world has become corrupt. It is because we are still on the same old ground, still feeding on the same old patch. Still on the same claim staked out by Christian Platonism, Christian idealism. All our discoveries are confined to the few remaining hollows and odd parts by chance left uncharted; all our advances in thought are lucky discoveries of the few avenues left still unexplored to their logical ends. Everything we do is still on the same worn-out plane which has been lived and relived till there is nothing left of it except what has gone rotten with use.

It is just as he said in *The Crown*: '*Whatever single act is performed by any man now, in this condition, it is an act of reduction, disintegration. The scientist in his laboratory, the artist in his study, the statesman, the artisan, the sensualist obtaining keen gratification. . . . Dmitri Karamazov . . . Dostoievsky has shown us perfectly the utter subjection of all human life to the flux of corruption.*

'Of course, no doubt any way of life, any created way of life – life-mode – is subject to this corruption. The state of analytic disintregation after the synthesis of dynamic creation. Even the dark, aboriginal way of life to which, as the furthest removed from my own, I am so drawn, even that has its process of corruption – sensual corruption as opposed to our Northern way of intellectual corruption. Both are parasitic on a way of life rather than creative of life for themselves.'

So in this book Lawrence applies a new criterion;

not the standard of lack of centrality, but the criterion of the effect of this lack, corruption. He describes his men and women either as part of the corrupting processes of the world, or as able to stand apart, with the ability to create themselves into a new way of life.

As a component of the general process of disintegration he describes Gerald, typical of the 'blond, Northern' way of corruption. He is tall and splendid, a fair-haired Englishman – brave and capable, able to control a great mining works, able to hold a company of people together and take charge of them by his personality, magnificent horseman, strong swimmer, never at a loss, and among women *my word he came out like a dandelion in the sun! He's a whole saturnalia in himself, once he is roused . . . he seems to reap the women like a harvest.* But it is no good his trying to make sure of himself like this, by being a Don Juan, going from one woman to another and trying to feel himself safe in them. He is never at rest. His tremendous 'go,' what happens to it? As the book proceeds, Gerald *experiences more and more a sense of exposure . . . when he was alone in the evening and had nothing to do, he had suddenly stood up in terror, not knowing what he was.* It was all right, he was an ordinary healthy modern young man – not ordinary, much above the average in attainments.

Yet all the time he felt a *faint, small but final sterile* horror. He gets momentary relief from Gudrun – *into her he poured all his pent-up darkness*

and corrosive death, and he was whole again; yet
almost at once his love turns to a sort of desire to
be sheltered by her, even be mothered by her. He
knows it only needs an effort of will to make him
isolated and impervious once more, but he cannot
make it because he has no real wants; he is already
dead, or that part of life is dead from which wants
come. And when, finding Gudrun unfaithful to
him, he walks off into the snow of the Alps and is
killed it is not suicide but the finish of a process.
His whole life has been a condition of death.

He is brought back frozen, ice, the end of the
Northern way of corruption.

Gudrun is to be typical of the other way, the
'sensual mode.' She is beautiful and accomplished,
clever in her work — she is an artist. *But always this
desolating, agonising feeling, that she was outside of
life.* She cannot take even her art seriously — *she
feels she might give herself away.* Like Gerald she is
commanding and imperious and attractive, and spas-
modically abandons herself to 'orgiastic passion';
but she has no real quietness — there is really nothing
there, no Gudrun, and she realises it lying alone in
her room. *The thought of the mechanical succession
of day following day, following day, ad infinitum, was
one of the things that made her heart palpitate with a
real approach of madness.* Like Gerald, she was too
strong to take refuge in illusion and imaginations.
*Perhaps it was only her unabateable honesty that left
her so exposed to the truth.* Then she longs for someone, but not Gerald. *Why wasn't there somebody who*

E

would take her in their arms, and hold her to their breast, and give her rest, pure, deep, healing rest. But not Gerald – he needed somebody to help him in the same way. She did not know whom she wanted.

That the whole world is not going the way of corruption along with Gerald and Gudrun, Lawrence makes clear by presenting himself in the book in the persons of Birkin and Ursula. For besides wanting to account for the world and the wrong in it from which he has suffered, Lawrence accounts for himself. Gerald dies, Birkin does not die. Immortality is a question of character. Birkin has roots; he has the power to recreate himself out of the elements into which, as part of the corruptive process of modern life, he too is disintegrating.

Women in Love describes the process of his renewal. Lawrence, in this book and in the *Fantasia*, has sufficiently made up his mind about the experience of *Look We Have Come Through* to be able to explain it as evidence of his difference from the world he attacks.

In the beginning of *Women in Love*, Birkin is a part of the general corruption in which the other characters are fixed. He is far from 'all right.' *At least my only rightness lies in the fact that I know it, I detest what I am outwardly. I* LOATHE *myself as a human being*. Outwardly – but inside him there is something which makes him different from the others, a warmth and vulnerability, a lack of hardness. It was true something made him spend time with Hermione and the thing she stood for. Something in common with her, of course – some spirituality. But he *knew* it. '*He knew that his spirituality was concomitant of a process of depravity, a sort of pleasure in self-destruction. There really was a certain stimulant in self-destruction. . . . But then he knew it.*

Knowing it in Birkin's sense of the word 'know' made it possible for him to save himself; *and he who was so near to being gone with the rest of his race down the slope of mechanical death* is ultimately rescued by his contact with Ursula. Sexual contact, but how different from Ursula's with Skrebensky, or Gudrun's with Gerald.

Birkin knows that whereas there is no real Gudrun, there is a real Ursula, and to get at this Birkin tries to approach her without there being preconceptions of love and sex on her side or his. She tries to insist that it is love. What is there beside? *Why, there is a final me which is stark and impersonal and beyond responsibility: so there is a final you. And it is there I would want to meet you . . . not a mingling, but an equilibrium, a pure balance of two single beings.*

During the course of the book, after many battles, Birkin achieves this. He has lived the sexual experience; that is why he has not *used* sex for gratification or as a means to children or as a means to calm away feelings of insufficiency. On the contrary he has experienced it as part of something greater, and through it has gained knowledge of another person. *Never to be seen with the eye, or known with the mind, only known as a palpable revelation of living otherness.*

So Lawrence makes clear the Lawrence of *Look We Have Come Through.* Now he can describe it – how that through this experience he can create himself. He can and will set it forth, so that others may know what is to be done, so that the world may be saved, and he may not be engulfed again with the others. There will be sneers by young modern Bohemians and dilettantes at the Café Royal – indeed he shall be beforehand in this, and describe such criticisms in his book. 'Salvator Mundi.' . . . 'It is *himself* is corrupt – him a saviour!' Well, let them sneer. He *will* alter the world, he will make it impossible for himself to be touched again, as he was, by the war and the people who ran it.

In an essay book, the *Fantasia of the Unconscious*, whatever ground he has left uncovered in *Women in Love* he deals with. Modern science, modern intellectualism, modern education. All these he explains as the more obvious aspects of disintegration – mechanical and dead. In their place he composes a new science, morphology and cosmogony of his own. It all forms a kind of metaphysic, more definitely explanatory, even, than *Women in Love*: for Lawrence still feels *the absolute need which one has for some sort of satisfactory mental attitude towards oneself.*

And, of course, towards European sciences – the

need to put them down, to show how they are all sciences of the old dead world: *even biology never considers life, but only mechanistic functioning and apparatus of life*. All analysis and corruption. So I must account for things in a living way, construct a science in living terms, however great the apparent contradiction. Something much more like the old Greek philosophers – Heraclitus – something with more of alchemy in it, where there is mystery instead of mechanisation.

I honestly think that the great pagan world of which Egypt and Greece were the last living terms, the great pagan world which preceded our own era, once had a vast and perhaps perfect science of its own, a science in terms of life. Who knows – perhaps astrology has roots in something more than superstition? *Perhaps I have the seed of Mars in my veins.* That war-god had nothing to do with what we call war. Our war – Yes, now at last I understand the war – was the most completely mechanical thing that has happened. . . . Indeed it did *not* happen, not *to me or to any man in his own self. It took place in the automatic sphere, like dreams do. But the actual man in every man was just absent – asleep.* I would fight. I would kill my enemy. *But become a bit of that huge obscene machine called war, that I would never do.*

I never will – because I will never let it happen again, and over and beyond all explanations and interpretations this is the fact that I will maintain and maintain and maintain: that *we must realise fully, and then make up our minds. The war was foul, as long as I am a man, I say it and assert it, and further I say, as long as I am a man such a war shall never occur again. It shall not and it shall not.*

§4. THE FAILURE OF FRIENDSHIP

['Aaron's Rod']

THE war behind him, Lawrence, the new Lawrence, as he believes, is ready for new action. He is very clear, now, that his successful marriage must inaugurate an entirely new sort of activity. Hitherto he has only been explaining what has already happened. *Sex* (and the explanation of it) *as an end in itself is disaster . . . and there can be no successful sex union unless the greater hope of purposive, constructive activity fires the soul of the man all the time.*

Successful sex union is to be followed — by what? New activity. In what direction?

All my life I have wanted friendship with a man — real friendship, in my sense of what I mean by that word. What is this sense? Do I want friendliness? I should like to see anybody being 'friendly' with me. Intellectual equals? Or rather equals in being non-intellectual? I see your joke. Not something homosexual, surely? Indeed you have misunderstood me — besides this term is so imbedded in its own period. I do not belong to a world where that word has meaning. Comradeship perhaps? *No*, not that — too much love about it — no, not even in the Calamus sense, not comradeship — not Manly Love. Then what Nietzsche describes — 'the friend in whom the world standeth complete, a capsule of the good — the creating friend, who hath always a complete world to bestow'? Well, in a way. That means, in my words, choose as your friend the

71

man who has centre. But this does not explain it. My next book will do this.

So far he had never enjoyed this friendship he wanted. There had been a moment with the young farmer, recorded in *The White Peacock*, but it had been mostly hanging back from the real thing which Lawrence wanted.

One of the main issues of *Women in Love*, the one stressed on the last page, is the relation between Birkin and Gerald. In the first part of the book, it was apparently a relationship of talk and arguments about the mines, and 'religion,' and newspaper articles. *They really kept it to the level of trivial occurrence. Yet they burned with each other, inwardly.*

They became more and more friendly; but no — Birkin will not have this. *He knew that Gerald wanted to be fond of him without taking him seriously — and this made him go hard and cold.* Yet he was not really sure himself what it was he wanted. He had 'no certain belief in the possibility of any deep relationship between men.'

It is when he has got right with Ursula, when he feels that his life contact with her life will produce some living 'emergent value'; it is then that he casts round for some purpose to his activity. So far as he can tell he wants to repeat this contact experience with someone different, a man. With Gerald? He can find only immature words to express what it is he means. *Do I want a final, almost extra-human relationship with him — a relationship in the ultimate of me and him — or don't I?* Well, he does, he decides.

But at the last moment Gerald, like George, hangs back. He is always after Birkin and wants to feel he is there, believing him to be the only person he can 'talk to.' Yet there is one last barrier which will never fall. Birkin seems to think so, and even tries to break through this barrier by a sort of trick — by having a wrestling match with Gerald and struggling with him till both are exhausted and all reserve and self-consciousness is sent to sleep — till everything is lost except the sense of complete physical exhaustion and instincts of self-preservation. Fatally for himself, Gerald fails to respond.

But what is it exactly that Gerald is hanging back from? It is the one thing Lawrence leaves not accounted for. Still, Lawrence is beginning to know what it is he wants so that he can express it. Talking about Gerald after his failure and death, Birkin says: *'He should have loved me. I offered him.'* Why should? How loved? Offered what?

Lawrence writes the next book to explain. In *Aaron's Rod* Birkin, now Lilley, is given another potential friend, Aaron. Lawrence is able to say, now, how the 'real contact' works, or should work. The novel is the account of this new activity. The *Look We Have Come Through* experience is now definitely a thing of the past. Ursula has dwindled to a sceptical, unsympathetic wife Tanny, who scarcely appears at all. In fact he feels her faintly in the way of the new things he has to do. In another book he writes: *He knew that her greatest grief was when he turned away from their personal intimacy to this impersonal business of male activity for which he was always craving. Aaron's Rod,* rather than achieving friendship, is this activity.

To start with: *I don't have friends who don't fundamentally agree with me. A friend means one who is at one with me in matters of life and death.* First Lawrence describes Jim Bricknell, the man who is *not* at one with him on supreme matters. Jim Bricknell is confident and knowing and successful. Lilley's wife is deplorably attracted. Bricknell is breezy about how splendid Christ is. *Don't you think love and sacrifice are the finest things in life?* Bricknell is always eating, because he is beginning to feel conscious of the fact that he has nothing inside him. He is dissatisfied because he does not get such splendid love feelings as he used. You don't know what my sensations used to be like, he says to Lilley. *I used to get the most grand feelings — like a great rush of fire or light — right here, at the solar plexus.* There is an argument, and Bricknell, after punching Lilley in the wind, has as a result a rush of emotion for him. *I like him better than any man I've ever known, I believe.* But no: Lilley won't have this. It is emphatically not the kind of contact he wants. Bricknell is horrible and detestable. Lilley will never see him again.

He is not sure at first what to make of Aaron, though he finds him very interesting. Aaron has just left his wife and family, — because he *wants* to. Specifically, he left his wife because she bullied him, trying to turn him into her way of life. Aaron has

just gone off from them all. Now here *is* a fundamental agreement. Lawrence feels this is very
much what he might do himself.

However, Aaron, like Gerald, appears to hang
back. He wants bringing to the front. Lilley nurses
him through an illness, and after it they part more
suddenly than seems necessary; the whole thing is
left in the air. Lilley goes to Italy. Aaron stays
behind. *He knew perfectly well that Lilley had made
a certain call on his, Aaron's, soul: a call which he,
Aaron, did not intend to obey.*

Nevertheless, after a time, Aaron goes to Italy
too — not to meet Lilley, but indirectly owing to
him.

When he gets there, an extraordinary change
begins in him. Is it the country? He looks round:
there seemed a new life quality everywhere. Like
Lilley, in a way, to be made to feel so by merely
changing countries. He goes to stay at a grand
house where Lilley is known, talked about, and run
down. For the first time in his life, Aaron feels the
necessity of taking sides — on behalf of his friend.
After he has left the house he writes a letter to his
host.

*I don't want my Fate or my Providence to treat me
well. I don't want kindness or love . . . I want the
world to hate me, because I can't bear the thought that
it might love me . . .* an extraordinary letter — really
Lawrence might almost have written it.

Near the end of the book, the two are together
again in Florence — no pre-arranged meeting. Aaron

has something to be worked out, a physical passion for a woman there, which is unsatisfactory — perhaps because the woman in her way insists on love as his wife had, perhaps because he is really married to his wife for good and can never be satisfactorily joined to anyone else. Aaron scarcely knows. He scarcely knows what to do; though he remembers things which Lilley has said about such situations: that husbands are husbands for ever, for instance, and that they can never be lovers. This is a great help; also the fact that Lilley is there, the fact that he is present in the town with him in some way gives him strength. He knows what to do, now, and does it, leaving this Italian woman as he had left his wife.

In the end of the book Aaron ceases struggling against Lilley: the perfect friendship is near achievement. Was Aaron to go on to some other woman, or go on being a 'success' with his charm and his music? *But no! If he had to give in to something: if he really had to give in, and it seemed he had: then he would rather give in to the devilish little Lilley than to the beastly people of the world . . . yielding to the peculiar mastery of one man's nature.*

And Aaron, yielding to this mastery and sitting, as it were, at Lilley's feet, listens while Lilley cheerfully but quietly tells him about life, about what 'being yourself' really means, about the two great dynamic urges. *Do you believe me? I don't care a straw. Only for your own sake, you'd better believe me* — the two great urges, love and power, and how

that the 'love urge' is expanded, and the time has
come for the 'power urge.'

Lilley talks quietly but cheerfully. *Remember
this, my boy: you've never got to deny the Holy Ghost
which is inside you, your own soul's self. Never, or
you'll catch it.* You've got to submit to what it says.
All men say they want a leader. *Then let them in
their souls* submit to *some greater soul than theirs.*

  — And whom shall I submit to?
  — Your soul will tell you.

Friendship, real contact between man? What a
strange turn it has taken during the progress of this
book. Aaron to submit to something in Lilley —
but what is Lilley to submit to in Aaron? Where
is the essential *mutual* nature of friendship — the
mutual exchange of worlds? Well, Lawrence seems
to say, why not admit it? I am of a different order —
a new order of being. That is why there can be
nothing mutual about it. I am here to lend out
my power to those who are in need of it.

Is this friendship? Lawrence himself begins to
wonder. Are Lilley and Aaron friends? Perhaps
that is not what Lawrence wants at all?

Lawrence has to admit to himself that Aaron
never existed, at any rate not the Aaron who sits
at Lilley's feet. Jim Bricknell does. They all
seem to be Jim Bricknells — Lawrence is glad he
has got them so well in that chapter about him.
But where is the right man? Friendship has been
a failure; his new activity — what will happen to it?

It is all right; he has known all along that friendship was the wrong word. *Aaron's Rod* is no sooner finished than he understands where the last part of it is leading: then he realises its full implication. *All his life he had cherished a beloved ideal of friendship — David and Jonathan.* Now he knew *he did not want friendship or comradeship, great or small, deep or shallow.*[1] Some other relationship. But what?

'Whom shall I submit to?' Aaron had said.

'Your own soul will tell you.'

The mystery of lordship.

Aaron looked up into Lilley's face. It was dark and remote seeming — it was like a Byzantine eikon.

The book written, Lawrence now knows — for certain — his real destiny.

[1] Kangaroo.

['Kangaroo']

To get free of his past life, to make sure that his newly realised destiny as leader will be given the best chance, Lawrence leaves Europe and goes to a new continent – Australia, the newest and most free of them all. He becomes more and more anxious to get on somewhere else. From England to Italy, from Italy to Sicily, from Sicily to the Black Forest. He will never, if he can help, return to any place, particularly if it has been the scene of vivid experience. England least of all. Sometimes it becomes almost like the cry of Masha in the *Three Sisters* – 'To Moscow – if only we could go to Moscow': except that Lawrence does act on his impulse. Now he wants to leave Europe behind, and the rest of his past life with it. *I feel Europe becoming like a cage to me. Europe may be all right in herself. But I find myself chafing. Another year I shall get out.*

This is from *Aaron's Rod*. In less than a year he is out of Europe – in India first, but there nothing seems to happen. Presumably he only finds the end of another stream of culture, stages further gone in corruption even than Europe itself. He goes on to Australia.

In Australia he finds just what he has wanted. The expanse is so vast it almost frightens him: yet everything is new. The look of the moon and the quality of the sun, the new plants and the curious animals, the air, which seems unbreathed and untouched. The famous extraordinary bush, also, which seems so quiet and in a way dead and yet waiting — for what? To be created? It certainly seems the place for him.

Lawrence decides to stay. After getting the 'feeling' of Australia by living in the Western uninhabited parts, he settles in Sydney. A rather dreary suburban district; still, this can be magnificently described, and he has a feeling that if he stays in one of the principal Australian towns for three months — he sets himself three months — something will come of it. He is now sure of himself as a potential leader, though he put it, at first, more impersonally. He is now sure that *power* is the thing: that *there must be one who urges, and one who is impelled.* Later on he becomes more definite. *As a man who is by nature an aristocrat it is my sacred duty to hold the lives of other men in my hands.*[1] And here in Sydney, well, he can only wait, at present. So far as authority goes, incidentally, there seems to be none. Everything appears to be run without any bossing, and it is all very easy-going. There was too much equality altogether, in a rather forced, socialist 'I'm-as-good-as-you' way.

Things developed quickly and unexpectedly, from the direction of his next-door neighbours — young married couple. The husband had been interested in Lawrence and his wife (now Somers and Harriet) since their first coming. They start

[1] Dionys, in *The Ladybird*.

visiting each other, and soon, in the midst of general talk, Jack begins 'sounding' Somers on what he thinks about things — about Australia, and about its future, and about its politics.

'At any rate *politics* won't help,' says Somers, 'sounding' in his turn.

This put them off.

But what *will* help? If you don't believe in politics what *do* you believe in? Do you care about anything?

Why, yes, I care supremely.

About what?

That you either know or you don't know, and if you don't know, it would only be words my trying to tell.

Somers bides his time. Conversations between Jack and Somers continue. Somers's wife doesn't like this earnest talking in which she does not take part. 'Why do you talk to him? He's only an ordinary bumptious young Australian.' Somers, answering her, talks to himself: *I want to do something with living people, somewhere, somehow, while I live on the earth. I write, but I write alone. And I live alone. Without any connection whatever with the rest of men.*

Therefore when Jack breaks the secret to him, Somers pays great attention. There is a movement on foot, more political, certainly, than religious, but emphatically outside Socialism or Capitalism or Nationalism. A movement started partly to save Australia from the coldness and tyrannies of just such issues.

F

Somers feels drawn. Jack says they all swear to obey their leaders, it is a movement of men wanting to obey *leaders*. . . .

Somers shakes hands on it. Jack is ecstatic. Somers feels hopeful. Is this his opportunity? Yet *why did his heart feel heavy? Politics — conspiracy — political power: it was all so alien to him. Yet Australia, the wonderful . . . it might begin here.*

True they have their leader already, Kangaroo; but Somers meets him, and is swept off his feet by admiration. An extraordinary man, ugly, like a kangaroo, but what force, what command. He has read Somers's books and welcomes him as at least an equal. Somers has never seen anyone like him. *He was almost purely kind, essential kindliness embodied in an ancient, unscrupulous shrewdness.* Somers is charmed, and much impressed. There seems real agreement between them, too. Kangaroo speaks of the need of submitting, and the need of being relieved of authority. Splendid sentences he speaks — *The Ten Commandments which Moses heard was the very voice of life. But the tablets of stone he engraved them on are millstones round our necks.*

Somers is carried away. But when he has left Kangaroo there is a reaction. Is it that there is *too much* force, too much warmth? He goes off and looks at the sea, and suddenly feels that he does not care what Kangaroo says, or what anybody says. *He felt almost fiercely cold. He liked the sea, the pale sea of green glass that fell in such cold foam. Ice-cold, fish-burning.* Too much warmth, is it?

Too much leadership, perhaps? Too much warmth, certainly. *Who sets a limit to what a man is?* He doesn't want to be permanently led towards warmth, and rightness — certainly not by Kangaroo. Too much leadership.

Somers and Kangaroo, after their first meeting, do not get on. Somers is himself a great leader, or about to be one — and here is Kangaroo taking him confidently to his bosom as if he was already certain of his coming in with him. As a disciple, it would be. He has tried to lead Lawrence — and even, for a moment, carried him away. *No*, Lawrence won't be 'influenced,' and if anyone tries to do it, he can show how absurd it would be.

To lead him who has got beyond all leaders. Others have been leaders to him in the past it is true — Nietzsche, Dostoievsky, Christ, Whitman — and see how he has got beyond them, how he sees where they are wrong. Nietzsche for instance, when he talks of power he means intellectual power, mental power, conscious will-power. 'I mean something far deeper than that. Dostoievsky — I have explained him too: how sensual gratification is made a goal with him — the sensual gratification of analysis — and of course his kind of Christianity is the key to him. Christ was a great leader to me once, but no, He is not for me now. Too much universality. *A man should remain himself, not try to spread himself over humanity.* Even Whitman, I can acknowledge the valuable part in him and yet he can never be a leader to me after what I now know and have experienced of integrity and isolation — he will never lead me, with his *En Masse,* *Democracy, One Identity.* . . . Too much universality again.'

Somers now knows that this is what is wrong with Kangaroo, and in dramatic scenes he tries to tell him. An extraordinary issue, two leaders both insisting on being leaders and on not being led. Kangaroo will not yield, and Somers begins to hate him. Kangaroo, on the other hand, loves Somers, and the more he tries to be the leader by loving, the more Somers tries to be the leader by refusing to be loved. Kangaroo yearns over him, speaking, not exactly to Somers, but to the void — until at last he sees it is no use and stands with his head down, his back to Somers. Somers, hating back, thinks to himself, '*If I were a kestrel I'd stoop and stick him straight in the back of the neck and he'd die. He ought to die.*'

They part, after a quarrel in which Kangaroo says some 'unworthy' things — Somers gets at least that satisfaction. But he has been no leader to Kangaroo.

The next thing is that Jack and his friends turn bitterly against him. They love Kangaroo, and from regarding Somers as a possible co-leader, they begin to mistrust and avoid him.

So this first attempt at fulfilling his destiny as a leader has been a failure. As he stays on it becomes more and more hopeless for him even to think of leadership in Australia. Besides, his desire to lead has gone. He knows, in his present state, he cannot do it. He cannot even be leader to his wife, who refuses to accept him at all as 'lord and master' — and it is part of what he has always maintained, that *women must submit to the positive power-soul in man, for their being.*

Somers feels pulled down by the Kangaroo affair; and he is frightened into a sort of police fear by Jack and the others who are almost threateningly disappointed in him. He is reminded of his feelings in the war and thinks them out and out. He goes all through it. He must get rid of it finally — indeed he thought he had. He must get rid of his rages and hate. *For there was no digesting it. He had been trying that for three years, and roaming the face of the earth trying to soothe himself with the sops of travel and new experience and scenery.*

Now he really believed he should be getting rid of it. He had nearly let it sweep him away. Now he really must stand out of it finally. If only certain people would leave him alone, and certain other people would really believe in him, he was sure the devil inside him, *the black poisonous bud would burst into a lovely new, unknown flower.* He was certain of the things inside him — that *Look We Have Come Through* was what he had always thought it, *that the dark god in her* — his wife — *answering the dark god in me has got my soul heavy and fecund with a new sort of infant. But even now I can't bring it forth. I can't bring it forth.*

What was it? Did he perhaps himself still stand in need of a leader? He could not admit this. 'Living from the source.' This phrase had meaning to him, he could recognise the power to do this in others – in animals, for instance. Why should he, of all people, be so frustrated? Why was everything he did tinged with a kind of failure – not only this last business of being a leader, but his efforts towards friendship as well. His failure in sexual experience he had surmounted, but even the relation with his wife had not been perfect.

Lawrence was beginning to know what it was. There was something he was denying: *he kicked against the pricks. He did not yet submit to the fact which he half knew: that before mankind would accept any man for a being, and before Harriet would even accept him, as lord and master, he . . . who was so strong on kingship, must open the doors of his soul, and let in a dark Lord and Master for himself, the dark God he had sensed outside the door.*

It had always, he thought, been at the back of his mind. Now for a final acceptance of it. The dark god.

Lawrence leaves Australia at the end of the book. Somers and Harriet sail away for ever. The act of leadership has been a failure.

Nevertheless, he has learned this from it. He knows now, with certainty, and is able to decide, for the last time, what he must do. The most important and essential of all the new things that have been going to happen.

First of all, he must get right away to a new country.

§6. THE CLIMAX

['The Plumed Serpent']

As Somers said to himself, *Draw your ring round the world*, the ring of your consciousness.

This is to be the climax, this must be the climax, when I reach America, the new world which still remains. Even before he went to Australia he had thought of America as the real place for him: he knew of course that there all the European idealism he hated was to be found in its most rancid form, but he did not think of America as the United States; he thought of it as a huge continent with a huge meaning of its own, far stronger than the overflow of Europeanism lapping over part of it. He would go to Mexico, where there was still some of the Aztec blood: there he hoped to find the real life of the continent. *I can't do with folk who team by the billion*, he had said in the past. *Like the Chinese and Japs and Orientals, I would have loved the Aztecs and the Red Indians. I* know *they hold the element in life which I am looking for.*

'To look for a new element in life — the phrase used in *Aaron's Rod* — is I see now a truer way of putting it than "desire of friendship" or "leadership."' He has known all along, of course, that he was never meant to lead in the sense of being a 'famous leader of men,' a Cæsar. Cæsars are only instruments. He is going to lead, but indirectly, as the man who reveals the life mystery and by his act of revelation creates a new possibility, a strange

element in life. This is what my struggles connected with a 'dark god' have all led up to. But
why call it a god? Why have gods? Well, because
I have now come to · believe that *there must be
manifestations.*

Moreover my gods will not be anthropomorphic
gods so much as theomorphic men. And here
Mexico itself helps me so much — the names and
rituals and general character of the old Aztec gods
are all so adaptable to the god-like men I am creating
as the concrete embodiments of my revelation. In
their qualities and manifestations they are so utterly
different from the old northern deities for which I
have such a distaste; in their character — especially
that of the war-god Huitzilopochtli — so far removed from the effete mildnesses of all modern
religions. True, according to Prescott their worship
was accompanied by cannibalism and human
sacrifice on a gigantic scale, but who can say he
understands the institution of human sacrifice and
the mysterious function of the life mystery which
may have been fulfilled in the act? There is a
prophecy that their chief god, Quetzalcoatl, shall
return. Well, I am the John the Baptist of the
return. Or I am Quetzalcoatl incarnate if I allow
myself, if I allow the god part of myself to be fulfilled as it has always needed. Or at any rate I can
be Huitzilopochtli, the war-like supporter and
lieutenant. I will adopt the rich Mexican customs,
the splendid physical dances, the beautiful clothes,
and describe them against the background of this

strong blazing tropical country. I know they are
gods that I myself would have followed — they are
so unconnected with the old me the last remnants
of which I hope now finally to have shed. Certain
things in the Aztec religion — the importance of the
earth, for instance — seem made to express the vivid
effects which the objects of the earth, the surfaces
of the world, have on me. My sermons would not
aim to make the spirit seem real. There have been
enough metaphors for the spirit already. It would
speak more of the body and the earth. I, if anyone,
could write such sermons. *The snake of the world is
large, and the rocks are his scales, trees grow between
them. So vast a serpent you walk on, this lake lies
between his folds as a drop of rain in the folds of a
sleeping rattlesnake. . . . From the roots of his scales
we dig silver and gold, and the trees have roots in him,
as the hair of my face has root in my lips.* My commandments shall not be to the spirit to make
decisions for the future, but to the whole person
to make possible the existence in the present *moment*
of the body and the person of which it is part: *and
say to thy strength: Lo, the night is foaming up my
feet and my loins, day is foaming down from my eyes
and my mouth to the sea of my breast. Lo, they meet!*
But in this book the body is not to be more
stressed than the spirit. The two halves of the world,
the one of which I have always championed against
the other, I shall now, in evidence of my new whole-
ness, express as two factors of one unity. There
again — the name Quetzalcoatl! The Bird-Serpent,

it means. The feathered serpent — junction in a god of the bird of the air and the serpent of the earth. Quetzalcoatl himself is 'Lord of the Morning Star' and this shall be my new name for the essence which my two worlds share in common; the essence of which they are both opposing manifestations, *the superb rich stillness of the morning star* as it shines in Mexico, *the poignant intermediate flashing its quiet between the energies of the cosmos.*

There is to be no more hate in this book — no more attacks on the corruption of Europe, and no more devastating portraits of 'centreless' people meaninglessly detached from life. Yet for the sake of the novel there will be the theme of a woman, Kate — an Ursula, whom the Lawrence of the book, Cipriano, wants to marry and for whom Kate, before she is ready, has to disentangle herself bit by bit from the last strands of her 'humannesses' and ego and old European associations. There is the drama of her struggling to keep clear of and struggling at the same time to keep in last regretful contact with these entanglements. She is *almost* as ready to abandon herself as Cipriano — '*now I have only one thing to do — not to get caught up in the world's cog-wheels any more, and not to lose my hold on the hidden greater thing.*' Yet she sometimes falters. Over the mystical tricks — that is what they seem — that Ramon and Cipriano play for instance. Praying by holding up one arm above their heads and letting conscious thoughts lapse. It all seems like that man in England who has such an influence on people.

She says she *never understood mystical things.* '*They make me uneasy.*'

Is it mystical when I come in to you, Cipriano asks.

— *No, only physical.*

— *So is this, only further.*

Sometimes Kate feels that Mexico and the whole story of the revival of the gods and the fact of these two men identifying themselves with their particular deities — sometimes it seems unnatural and fantastic. *Mexico is really a bit horrible to me.*

'*Why not,*' says Cipriano. '*Horror is real. Why not a bit of horror, as you say among all the rest? . . . Get used to it that there must be a bit of fear, and a bit of horror in your life.*'

Nevertheless her superficial self fights a losing battle with these two men.

But there are no Geralds to balance Ramon Quetzalcoatl. There are no Jim Bricknells. Lawrence, in his climax book, feels he has no need to think about Jim Bricknells any more. He will not think of them. To Lawrence there is more of horror in the countenancing of such *men* than in the apprehension of gods. He has gone beyond them. After all, men are like monkeys. Ramon agrees with Kate.

Men are like monkeys. . . . One must be able to disentangle oneself from persons, from people. . . . In some way humanity dominates your consciousness. So you must hate people and humanity, and you want to escape. But there is only one way of escape, to turn beyond them.

Kate succeeds in going beyond 'people' and beyond herself. The last chapter of *The Plumed Serpent* is called 'Here.' Her hankering for London is gone. As she has said all along, she has only been superficially unwilling. *Now I have only one thing to do — not to get caught up into the world's cog-wheels any more.* Now she has succeeded in shedding completely her old life. Kate shall stand for Lawrence. He has been able to do this. *Ye must be born again.* . . . *Out of the fight with the octapus of life, the dragon of degenerate or incomplete existence, one must win this soft bloom of being.*

It is the climax book. *Here* for Kate is to mean *here* for Lawrence as well. It celebrates his escape from the octopus. There is to be no more hate for him, no more kicking against the pricks, only a fulfilment.

EPILOGUE

LAWRENCE comes to a stop with *The Plumed Serpent*. Books appear with the same regularity. . . . But the chief problem of Lawrence seems to be the question of this climax: how much it represents a real emergence into new life.

Did Lawrence really 'find God' in New Mexico? That there was nothing sudden about it, no sterile, sceptical Saul period followed by a blaze up, a vision, and a Paul period of fixed belief — that he has none of the esotericism of those who have had this 'mystical experience' but that on the other hand the 'dark god' of Lawrence has been slowly coming and has been making more and more frequent appearances in his work; and further the possibility that 'dark god' may be another name for what hitherto he has expressed as a concrete desire for new activity — these facts go to support the impression that there is a sense in which Lawrence always 'finds god,' a sense in which 'god' (or 'the god flame,' as he expresses it) appears in all his work.

But as to final fulfilment, for evidence of that there are the books which followed *The Plumed Serpent* to go to. Does his writing now take on a new positive quality, is there implied conviction, as distinct from expressed asseveration, which is the great general characteristic of the work — especially the fragmentary work — of Goethe, or the *Song of Myself*?

On the contrary, in his subsequent writing,

Lawrence seems in some ways to have gone back-wards.

So far from there being a new positive quality he takes old situations, allegorises them, and presents them twice as assertively. Hitherto, though the characters he describes may sometimes be hoisted out of reality to illustrate the point he wants to make, the issues in which they take part are obviously, in the main, the record of experience. His men and women are real enough to make it obvious when they cease to become real. Aaron is real, so that it is a shock when he suddenly turns into something Lawrence wants him to be. Gerald is real; there must, it is certain, be a Gerald in Lawrence himself. Even Hermione Roddice seems truly and imaginatively recorded. The issue between Kangaroo and Somers, the two leaders struggling to lead each other, is so obviously true that the downing of Kangaroo by Somers, and the set, victorious conclusion seems a natural part of the Lawrence-Somers character truthfully explained.

But since *The Plumed Serpent*, there has been a change.

Lady Chatterley's Lover, for example, the theme of which is the Lawrence triangle. The Lawrence triangle consists of the English-gentleman adoring *husband*, whose neo-platonist way of loving devastates the *wife*, who is frustrated by her lack of sensual fulfilment until she meets the *lover*, the Lawrence man, the antithesis in all respects to the husband, the satyr to his Hyperion. This situation

D. H. LAWRENCE 1929

from a Self Portrait

as treated by Lawrence in his short story *The Ladybird* has a reality quite apart from the auto-biographical truth of the main issue. The difference between the husband, Basil, and the lover, Count Dionys — the difference between his world of intelligent English country-house interest in things and willingness to talk, and the Count's passionate reserve, is a real difference quite independent of the categorical one implied. But in *Lady Chatterley* the husband and the lover are like personifications in a Tudor morality play. Clifford, the husband, wheels himself about in a chair, symbolically paralysed below the waist. Mellors, the gamekeeper and lover, the most abstract of all the 'Lawrence men' who continually speaks (and writes in his letters) pure Lawrence, has run the gauntlet of varied, if unsatisfactory sexual experience. He comes to a good end; whereas Clifford, it is indicated, comes to a bad one. Lawrence's criterion of the characters in this book depends neither on 'centrality' nor 'corruption,' but is one of pure downright black-or-whiteness. Lady Chatterley's sister, who is opposed to her going off with her gamekeeper, is written down pure white. Her cousin, the aristocratic Tommy Dukes, on the other hand, who says 'be damned to the artificial sex compulsion' is made as black as your hat and reminds Lady Chatterley strongly — she does not know why — of that interesting man she has never yet spoken to, her gamekeeper. We feel like complaining Isn't there some other side of the hard-and-fast English gentleman which Lawrence might show us? If we give him his point, that they have their highly undesirable qualities, will he now please re-create these men for us? And will he also, if he is as changed as he should be, show us the changed Lawrence man? 'Here is the vast importance of the novel, properly handled,' says Lawrence. 'It can inform and lead into new places the flow of our sympathetic consciousness, and it can lead our sympathy away in recoil from thoughts gone dead.'[1] Lady Chatterley, so far as its issues are concerned, has just this deadness.

In the light of these resuscitations (the same sort of restatement of old things appears in most of the short stories of *The Woman Who Rode Away*[2]) *The Plumed Serpent* appears in a new light. It can so easily be interpreted, for instance, as a sort of 'wish-fulfilment' book, an idealisation of Lawrence's own life. Lawrence himself idealised as Cipriano, the great leader, the respected general, in touch with life in every sense; Lawrence's struggles with his own frustrations and doubts idealised in Cipriano's direct contact with his dark god, personified as Ramon; Somers's trouble with the wife who will not take him seriously enough idealised in Kate's ultimate acknowledgment of Cipriano. One begins satirically to think what *did* happen in New Mexico.

---

[1] *Lady Chatterley's Lover.*
[2] Even the eloquent *Pansies* is a rich filling out of the old Lawrence, with vivid attacks on 'chemicalised women,' 'wimbly-wambly young men,' and workmen 'living like lice.'

And then it could be said – Idealism is exactly what Lawrence, at his coming-of-age, wanted to get away from: and now he has come round to it again, his creativeness repressed in the creed of a new religion. It must be because he was never able to get free from the idealism that held him down in his youth; that he has never been able to re-create that bit of himself which was created for him by his environment.

'I reckon a crow is religious, when he sails across the sky,' he says in *Sons and Lovers*. He has altered since then.

Yet this doesn't 'account for' Lawrence any more than the various psycho-pathological explanations which will suggest themselves 'account for' him. A crow is doubtless religious when it flies across the sky. So may Lawrence well be when he is struggling with his conscience – with his passion, that is, for with Lawrence his passion and conscience are one. He is behaving, like the crow, as a unit of urgent life. There is never any doubt about the living quality in Lawrence. The question is how does he express it.

The answer to this question comes so slick that we almost suspect it: namely, that the evidence of the reality of D. H. Lawrence lies less in his successive judgments than in the new qualities of his own world set forth in the novels which form their background. 'The idea does not matter so much as the way it is expressed' is a blighting and very literary doctrine. Nevertheless when the idea – and

G

this is often the case with Lawrence — does not coincide with the experience, the way it is expressed is everything.

Yet this very idealogical side of Lawrence expresses his sincerity, but it is a less fundamental sincerity than that which he expresses when he describes himself in the person of characters who are incapable of sliding out of crucial situations — people like Aaron, or Jack in *Boy in the Bush* — people who try, and are sometimes able, to act in accordance with their real wants.

To express such a power is an achievement of infinite importance.   Even a man who only partly succeeds in this has a world to reveal: it now remains to describe the qualities of this world.

PART THREE
A WORLD

A WORLD

NEW QUALITIES. To become familiar with the work
of any creative artist is to become increasingly aware
that some new impression is gradually forming in
us: something like a new taste or a new smell —
something which we imagine could be summed up
in one word, if only it could be got at. The word for
Dante has something to do with vastness and brightness — but in no familiar sense. It is something
new done to the world, as Homer, for instance,
simplifies it, or Dostoievsky intensifies it, or Bee-
thoven floods it to the root. The more distinct the
effect the more elusive the word. What does
Mozart do for instance? He aerates it? But that
verb has formidable different associations. Bach
seems to stratify it —

New words would be wanted, for it is to describe
a new quality added to life.

What is the word for Lawrence? As his career
progresses, this 'one quality,' 'one savour,' becomes
more easy to separate out. It certainly has some
connection with *movement*. Well, so have all important new world-attributes — or at any rate with
displacement; with the dissolving, that is, of
crystallisations.

It is a special kind of movement in life, however,
which Lawrence gives. It may be called *flow
beneath the shape*. Or, to use a favourite word of
his, 'flux.' He is one to whom the πάντα ῥεῖ

concept is a concrete experience, and whatever he is writing about, this will come into it unmistakably somewhere.

It is not enough to say that in his world 'Things Flow.' That 'Things Flow,' that what appears to us static is 'really' in motion is not only one of the most ancient but also one of the most valuable of truths; it is, that is to say, a fact of the outside world which for a long time has lent itself fruitfully for expression by creative artists.

'That "all things flow" is,' as Whitehead says,[1] 'the first vague generalisation which the unsystematised, barely analysed intuition of men has produced. It is the theme of some of the best Hebrew poetry in the Psalms; it appears as one of the first generalisations of Greek philosophy'; it is found 'amid the barbarism of Anglo-Saxon thought.' But, he adds, 'without doubt, if we are to go back to that ultimate, integral experience, unwarped by the sophistications of theory, that experience whose elucidation is the final aim of philosophy, the flux of things is one ultimate generalisation around which we must weave our philosophical system.'

THE QUALITY IN PEOPLE. Lawrence is less objective. He does not weave a system. He shows, first, how this particular quality of reality is manifested in people. He concentrates not on talk and appear-

---

[1] *Process and Reality.*

ance but on the feelings, conscious and unconscious, that surge independently beneath. To do this seems strange in an English novelist. When Jane Austen is writing of persons, whether the passage is crucial or not, whatever she implies she certainly does not describe surge of feeling. When, for instance, Mr. Darcy leans forward to declare his passion for Elizabeth Bennett his rebuff is described like this:

> Elizabeth looked surprised. The gentleman experienced some change of feeling; he drew back his chair, took a newspaper from the table, and, glancing over it, said, in a colder voice:
> 'Are you pleased with Kent?'

I quote this simply because the method is quite in the English tradition, a charming example of it, and yet it would not be conservatively dogmatic to say that D. H. Lawrence is unlike Jane Austen in his way of writing here. After reading a crucial passage in one of his novels silly reminiscent parodies come into the mind. One thinks of how he would have treated the same incident. Elizabeth Bennett, while outwardly passive, would have felt the cold blood mounting through her veins in an agony of restive repulsion, an elaborate shock would have radiated outward and downward, in bright waves of repudiation. Darcy would know, in his soul, that she would not have him. Lawrence, in fact, would dwell on exactly what Jane Austen only implies: the unexpressed feelings.

There is a good example of this in *Aaron's Rod* —

the effect on Aaron of being robbed. Aaron is conventionally speaking an unemotional man, yet we recognise the truth in this description:

> As he was going home, suddenly, just as he was passing the Bargello, he stopped. He stopped, and put his hand to his breast pocket. It was as if lightning ran through him at that moment, as if a fluid electricity rushed down his limbs, through the sluice of his knees, and out at his feet, leaving him standing there almost unconscious. . . .
>
> He had been robbed . . . and he had known it. When the soldiers jostled him so evilly they robbed him. He had known it as if it were fate. . . . Feeling quite weak and faint, as if he had really been struck by some evil electric fluid, he walked on. And as soon as he began to walk, he began to reason. Perhaps his letter-case was in his other coat. . . .

The Lawrence quality in people is brought out more indirectly, though more objectively, in another way. One of the old jokes against him is that his men are all thigh and his women all hip. It is his way of not concentrating on the face when he describes. He seems to feel that the gesture of the body is far more lucid, and that it has only become unexpressive stagnating beneath clothes. A man standing without clothes, Lawrence says somewhere, is like a tramcar stripped of its advertisements. Naked bodies are only undressed bodies nowadays, he adds. Nevertheless though in words we concentrate on the accepted face and hands, there is more communication, for Lawrence, in the whole body.

THE QUALITY IN RELATIONSHIPS. The mobility of
Person beneath the fixity of personal characteristics
is best brought out in Lawrence's way of stating
relationships. He makes two individuals talking and
looking across to each other over space seem one
organic whole with a flow of intercommunication
much stronger and more expressive than the words
and looks which interpret it. Far too powerful a
thing to be even affected, much less interpreted, by
speech. To Lawrence, this 'flow between' is the
important thing; and knowing his own power of
calling it into consciousness, he likes to explain it
sometimes as a new science, an addition to human
knowledge, with new data. In the *Fantasia* he
works out a kind of anatomy of it. He tries, in a
kind of a morphology of centres of 'polarity' —
attraction and repulsion — to express anatomically
the ways in which people are connected. In particular, for instance, he explains what passes between
child and mother and the different but equally
important link between child and father — all existing
outside the region of conscious control, only damaged by deliberate interference, deliberate control,
or deliberate love. This is all in the fourth chapter
of the *Fantasia*.

The relatedness of things — everything connected
with everything, in the metaphor of gravity — is
an image of the Lawrence quality. He even creates
a sound cosmogony on this basis, which by completely contradicting all other theories of the
universe at least puts these pretentious things in

their place by demonstrating their personal and ephemeral nature. The cosmogony is to show the connecting flow between persons and 'inorganic' things – the sun, the earth, the moon. The sun 'is a thrusting up of our brightness,' the earth 'a thrusting down of our darkness.' He exemplifies what he says by descriptions of himself writing his book, sitting against a tree in the Black Forest. 'That's how I write about all these planes and plexuses – between the toes of a tree, forgetting myself against the great ankle of the trunk. And then, as a rule, as a squirrel is stroked into its wickedness by the faceless magic of a tree, so am I usually stroked into forgetfulness, and into scribbling this book. My tree-book, really.'

Squirrel-tree, tree-Lawrence, Lawrence-sun. This kind of relatedness is in the novels – it is explained in the *Fantasia*.

It is a way of saying that growth by knowledge is not to be gained by a concentrated stare at the object, but by something depending less on an act of volition – something more like permeation.

THE QUALITY IN DEATH. Is Lawrence able to see lives not as a succession of incidents but as one continuous shape? He tries to show the real direction of lives inside the outward course of events. Sometimes he represents the unfolding of a person as something quite distinct from outward speech, incidents and attitudes.

Perhaps this is the reason why he writes with apparent truth when he describes death. Not as a sudden event or portentous stroke of Fate, but as one of the symptoms of a general process, or the most obvious event in the stages of a decay begun always, in the Lawrence world, by a breaking away from life, from the life-stock. Why talk of deaths as taking place more at one moment than another? *The White Peacock* is a description of the death of George, though he is still existing at the end of the book. But it is a description of a life denier, a man who weakly disobeyed certain commands and therefore to Lawrence a description of death. A man dies because he wants to — like Gerald Crich, who dies, more exactly, because he always withholds himself from that real contact with people which would establish him. He closes himself to the source of life — a withering, bleaching, freezing process well described. The death of Kangaroo is a death of discouragement and lack of acceptance of the different world which Somers represents. In all these processes, besides the well described detail and circumstance of the actual facts of death, what is well defined is the unconscious will to die underneath the automatic external determination to keep alive.

When he writes of persons, then, Lawrence goes beneath the surface. People are all very human underneath: and underneath that, again, they aren't. A man makes new superficialities by making new depths. It is this new depth in Lawrence which makes him write dramatically. If drama is contest, the importance of the drama depends on the radical nature of that contest; and Lawrence's way of putting not virtue against vice, not human grace against human foible, but one life mode against another life mode is the best drama, and exciting creation.

'LAWRENTIOMORPHISM.' Here are all these characters in the novels with their highly developed capacity for feeling. Sometimes the criticism is made: There never were such people; or: This is Mr. Lawrence speaking in terms of himself, as if such a criticism was a disparagement. But — of course there never were such people, because Lawrence is a creator, and therefore, or i.e., there never was such a man as Lawrence. Moreover, each one of them certainly is described in terms of himself. The undesirability of anthropomorphism depends on the anthropos. If the man is a fixed character with a finished 'personality' he will only be printing off reproductions of his own dead image. But if he is full of unrealised selves, and able to reveal them, anthropomorphism will be this revelation — will be creation.

At the other end of this 'flowing quality' is a man of extreme physical sensibility.

In *Kangaroo* 'Somers' is compared with Jack, the young and somewhat insensitive Australian. 'The chief difference was that he [Somers] looked sensitive all over, his body, even its clothing, and his feet,

even his brown shoes, all equally sensitive with his
face. . . . Jack strode . . . whereas Somers put
down his feet delicately, as if they had a life of their
own. . . .'

This is very Lawrence-like. He feels in so many
ways and directions. Not only his readers but he
himself knows it. As usual he has described himself
theoretically – again in the *Fantasia*, drawing up a
new account of the senses. In it he lays the incidence
of importance less on the outside organs of sense than
on the centre to which they lead. To illustrate the
fact that he does not see with his eye only, in a detached dissecting glance, he says how 'the root of
conscious vision' is almost entirely in the breast. We
are straining ourselves to see, see too much in one
mode – 'to see, see, see, everything, everything
through the eye, in one mode of objective
curiosity. . . .' The thought is good – how it
fits into his scheme does not matter: 'That is why
we wear glasses' – well, never mind the conclusion.

Lawrence also makes a difference between the
kinds of feeling peculiar to the different parts of the
body. The sense of touch is the one most starved in
us, he says, and speaks of four centres of feeling,
front and back, above and below. 'The breast touch
is the fine alertness of quivering curiosity, the belly
touch is a deep thrill of delight and avidity. . . . The
thighs, the knees, the feet, are intensely alive with
love-desire, darkly and superbly drinking in the
love-contact, blindly. Or they are the great centres
of resistance, kicking, repudiating . . . and the

teeth are the instruments of the sensual will . . . but we have forefeited our flashing sensual power.' The conclusion? That 'that is why we have false teeth,' of course. But never mind that. What is implied here is the quality of flow beneath shape is brought out by representing the potential fields of sense lying unused beneath the surface feelings. The 'ought' lies in Lawrence's belief that these are numbed by modern sensationalism – have become, in fact, little more than the ideas, the ghosts, of themselves.

THE QUALITY IN THINGS. This quality is given further value in Lawrence's description of things. First by means of his simple experience of the πάντα ρει concept. To explain how Lawrence brings out the quality of movement in 'static' objects is not easy. Perhaps this should come under the heading 'Lawrence's descriptive power.' But 'good descriptive writers' are either only good at producing effective approximations to preconceived pictures of things, or else they do not get their effect by describing the outside object itself. In effect they first show what they themselves are like, and then place the objects in this context. Once the new person appears, it only remains to say the words – to say *tree*, *star*, *roadway*, and these things are seen in a new light.

The floor-men forcing the planks close to be nail'd,
Their postures bringing their weapons downward on the bearers,
The echoes resounding through the vacant building.

Whitman has only to mention these things, and, knowing him, we seem to have found them newly described. It is the writer who conceals himself, who keeps himself very much out of it, who needs always, however familiar he may be with his art, to struggle to think out the exact right word to avoid the *cliché*. Yet the man who uses it, not the word itself, determines whether or not an expression is hackneyed.

Describing a journey through mountains, Lawrence speaks of the 'living' rock. Quite an uninteresting adjective in itself, but in the context of his work it suggests the creatable and godlike essence of the 'dead' material as compared with a certain used and unresponsive texture in human beings.

Sometimes Lawrence brings out the fluid quality more specifically. Paul Morel describes one of his pictures to Miriam in this way: '. . . as if I'd painted the shimmering protoplasm in the leaves and everywhere, and not the stiffness of the shape. That seems dead to me. Only this shimmeriness is the real living. . . .'

But how can this essence be brought out in words? In this way.

Lawrence describes a bull.

> A wall, a bastion,
> A living forehead with its slow whorl of hair.
> And a bull's large, sombre, glancing eye
> And glistening, adhesive muzzle. . . .
> Knowing the thunder of his heart
> And the roar of black bull's blood in
> The mighty passages of his chest.

In the account quoted a few pages back, of himself writing his book in the middle of the Black Forest, he describes the tree he is leaning against:

> I listen for their silence . . . it almost seems I can hear the slow, powerful sap drumming in their trunks . . . the powerful sap-scented blood roaring up the great columns. . . .

The shape is nothing. Lawrence emphasises this in another way — by describing total effect rather than ordered sense impression (the dark old Italian church, impregnated with centuries of incense, 'affected me like the lair of some enormous creature'), or by describing subjectively from the point of view of changing human emotions, suggesting by new examples the infinitude of differing realities beneath the shape. In *The Rainbow* Will and Anna visit Lincoln Cathedral. It is described first in respect of Will's confined religious emotion, and then it becomes Anna's revulsion from Will's attitude. Will saw it in one way — 'whether his soul leapt with the pillars upwards, it was not to the stars and the crystalline dark space, but to meet and clasp with the answering impulse of leaping stone, there in the dusk and secrecy of the roof. The far-off clinching and mating of arches, the leap and thrust of the stone. . . .'

This does not correspond with anything in Anna, so to her it is different.

'She, too, was overcome, but silenced rather than tuned to the place. . . . She caught sight of the wicked, odd little faces carved in stone, and she stood before them arrested. These sly little faces peeped out of the grand tide of the cathedral like something that knew better. They knew quite well, these little imps that retorted on man's own illusion, that the cathedral was not absolute. . . . Apart from the lift and spring of the great impulse towards the altar, these little faces had separate wills, separate motions, separate knowledge, which rippled back in defiance of the tide. . . .'

Two different cathedrals for two different natures.

'The grand tide of the cathedral' — there again is the flowing. Lawrence sees a bird sitting on a fishing-net in Mexico, 'red as a drop of new blood from the arteries of the air.'

Fix your eye on the object says Wordsworth. *Fix body and soul* says Lawrence.

Lawrence 'sees more in things than meets the eye' — that is to say things are symbols to him; yet they are symbols not of extraneous ideas but of their own essence. 'Symbol' is perhaps the wrong word. When he describes cypresses at Fiesole, he does not 'make them a symbol' of the lost Etruscan race.

> Tuscan cypresses . . .
> Folded in like a dark thought
> For which the language is lost . . .
> Is it the secret of the long-nosed Etruscans?
> The long-nosed, sensitive footed, subtly smiling Etruscans,
> Who made so little noise outside the cypress groves?
> They are dead . . .
> And all that is left
> Is the shadowy monomania of some cypresses
> And tombs.

H

He does not make a symbol of them. He disentangles from the cypresses this quality of Etruscan secrecy which has always been hidden in them.

One of the best descriptions is the whole of the chapter called 'Coal-dust,' in *Women in Love*. Gudrun and Ursula watch Gerald control his horse at a level-crossing as it flinches before the noises of a passing train. The motions of the mare – rebounding 'like a drop of water from hot iron'; the expression of the mastering Gerald, 'his face shining with fixed amusement'; the grindings of the goods train (described as it is to the mare, the buffers of the trucks striking horrifyingly). Then the whole scene is described along another dimension, built up on a new side by the description, as well, of the relationships concerned in the scene – the relation between Gerald and his horse, and the relationships which the incident brings out between Ursula – Gudrun – Gerald.

Then, without bringing out anything in particular, is described the walk round of the two girls past miners' houses and the lustful comments of the Sunday afternoon colliers. Lawrence must seem to some to be at his best in these haphazard directionless accounts, where the only selection employed is the only one that matters – the selection of things experienced.

It is all like the poetic expression of certain modern philosophies. Whitehead, for instance, allowing concreteness only to this very flow between things, this very junction, this act of apprehension.

Lawrence is not so explicit, though he knows about it enough to say things like: 'We are transmitters of life, and when we fail to transmit life, life fails to flow through us . . . only man tries not to flow.'

DISTINCTIONS. It is said that a sign of genius is the ability to find apt analogies. But analogies illustrating a difference – not a similarity. The opposition between the scientist and the poet is misleadingly expressed by the words 'analysis' and 'synthesis.' Scientists analyse down into common constituents, making things fundamentally the same. Poets strike separate unities out of complex components, making things fundamentally different. Indeed to make these differences is the sign of the poet. Lawrence seems to have the power. By means of a partial achievement in self-knowledge, he seems to have gained an inkling of his own roots, a consciousness of the direction and trend of his life, which makes him able to know by association the roots and the analogous, though different, life directions of others. Everyone is possessed of the fact that these distinctions exist. It is another thing to know them, and it is worth seeing where Lawrence shows this knowledge.

MALE AND FEMALE. First there is evidence that Lawrence has experienced the fact of 'maleness' in himself, and, thereby, the different fact of 'femaleness'

is brought into his field of consciousness as well.
Lawrence often writes about this distinction – about
male and female modes of life, and the way, as it
seems to him, the functions and natural ten-
dencies of the two have become entangled. Of course
he *would* hate the clever, capable, social-minded
woman, and the complementary man who likes to
allow women to take a protective, mothering kind of
lead in public life. Yet he does not imply, in newspaper manner, that women should be 'womanly' and
men 'manly.' His objection comes from a different
cause.

He tries to specify it. For instance:

'Woman will *never* understand the depth of the
spirit of purpose in man, his deeper spirit. And
man will never understand the sacredness of feeling
to woman.' Talking and explanation do not affect
this difference, he says. '*Whatever* a man says, his
meaning is something quite different and changed
when it passes through a woman's ears.' Therefore
when men and women play each other's rôles and
speak each other's words there can be none of the
essential union of conscious and unconscious wants.
Whether Lawrence has 'deeply experienced his own
maleness' or not he sometimes writes in a real and
true way when his subject is women. One of his very
earliest reviewers thought he was one. The *Nation*,
February 25th, 1911, said:

'This novel [*The White Peacock*] is a characteristic specimen
of the modern fiction which is being written by the feminine
hand. . . .' Though there is undoubted cleverness in this

'piece of paulo-post impressionism which owes its origin to
Zola rather than to English sources it is evident not only that
the characters were spun in the author's brain', but also that
the author is a woman.

But though the author is not a woman and
probably does not even ask his wife lists of crucial
questions, he can describe the feelings of women in
a way which, though it is not founded on 'characteristics,' nevertheless seems true. They are not
written down womanly, nor imperious, nor fickle,
nor flighty. The whole character of Alvina Houghton – the 'Lost Girl' – never comes near these
headings. Yet it is true. There never was a *book*
character who was part old-maid doing dusty house
jobs and part with moods of ironical recklessness
and impulsiveness.

The talk between Ursula and Gudrun at the
beginning of their novel, with its curious hardness
and indifference; Anna Brangwyn giggling in the
church with Fred; at the end of *The Trespasser*,
Helena and her two friends going off together to
Cornwall with imitation-undergraduate jokes – it all
seems true, and especially true when he is describing
women in love. 'March' in *The Fox* for instance:
'"Don't try any of your tomfoolery on me," she says.

'"Why, it's not tomfoolery, it's not tomfoolery.
I mean it. I mean it. What makes you disbelieve
me?"

'He sounded hurt. And his voice had such a
curious power over her; making her feel loose and
relaxed. She struggled somewhere for her own

power. She felt for a moment she was lost — lost — lost. The word seemed to rock in her as if she were dying.' Here is this difference, Lawrence says. He will add: It must be acknowledged. Recognise the quality of male, and the quality of female, and learn to know the difference, as Anna knew the difference between herself and old Skrebensky, recognising his maleness in his 'lean, concentrated age, his informed fire, his faculty for sharp, deliberate response.' The male and female are two modes, and must be kept distinct.

CIVILISED: ABORIGINAL. Contrasted modes of racial consciousness is another distinction. The difference between the quality of life in the Aryan Western European man and that of other cultures.

'The Indian way of consciousness is different from and fatal to our way of consciousness. Our way of consciousness is different from and fatal to the Indian.'

This distinction is *not* based on an emotional idea that savages are fine, but on a sense of pure difference arising from knowledge. When Lawrence writes of members of a race not his own, his words show he has partly understood their nature. It is no idea of a noble-savage-living-in-Nature such as he satirises in his essay on de Crèvecœur. This love of earth and nature is all particularly intellectual — Aryan, as Lawrence implies when he describes the Mexican child throwing stones at a bird. 'He could

not see that the bird was a real living creature with
a life of its own. This, his race had never seen.
With black eyes they stared out on an elemental
world, where the elements were monstrous or
cruel, as the cold, crushing black water of the rain
was monstrous, and the dry, dry, cruel earth.'
They are not to be taken as simple-hearted whites,
nor has the word 'noble' anything to do with them.
Lawrence describes them in his Mexican books —
their indifference, their hopeless powerlessness
under white exploitation, their consequent steady
malevolence.

Before he goes to America he is describing
Italian and Sardinian peasants. He is drawn to
them — no need, nowadays, to say 'wish-fulfilment'
because he likes them. Yet it does soothe him that
they 'have never known the pert renascence Jesus.
. . . They have mediæval faces, *rusé*, never really
abandoning their defences for a moment, as a
badger or a polecat never abandons its defences.
There is none of the brotherliness and civilised
simplicity.' Lawrence does like the clothes they
wear, too, and can't help contrasting white Mexican
trousers tied in at the ankle, or floppy Corsican
caps, with the international collar and tie. That is
part of the iconoclastic twist he must give his way
of setting out his experience. But so far as 'going
back' is concerned:

> Whatever else the South Sea Islander is, he is centuries and
> centuries behind us in the life struggle, . . . we can't go
> back to the savages: not a stride. We can be in sympathy

with them. We can take a great curve in their direction, onwards. But we cannot turn the current of our life backwards, back towards their soft warm twilight.

ANIMALS. Animals in literature are almost always drawn in the flat:—E. M. Forster. It is true. Animals are described so as to fit types and characters which must be the constructions of human ways of thinking and can have no existence outside them. Not only are animals invariably anthropomorphised; they are generally divided into heroic and non-heroic. The heroes are the horse and the dog, who both happen to have spiritual, deep, rather idealistic eyes of the kind which would in men represent a spiritual, deep, rather idealistic temperament but which in horses and dogs of course represents nothing of the sort: conversely the animals most unlike a noble man in appearance, like pigs and snakes, are taken as the villains. The result of making animals into toy representations of human types is that we begin to think of them as childishly imitating us. They become charming and childish, and to see charm and niceness in animals becomes a sort of test of the appreciation regarded as necessary in a world which recognises however vaguely a very strong something in them to be admired and liked. Even imitated. We decide it must be a likeable quality — human, or naïve.

Lawrence strongly feels the significance of animals. To think of them as the superiors of men

is merely to invert the concept of straight-line progress. To know how they differ is to widen the
possibilities of our own lives. In respect, for
instance, of the completeness of their single actions.
The fullness of meaning in a cat's leap – crows
lifting from a field – a mare in its paddock making
a sudden canter for no reason.

The way to express the difference can never be
to make an Æsop's Fable out of it. A fox is never
cunning, it is fox-like. A cow is never placid, it is
cow-like. A jackal is never craven, it is being a
jackal.

Of all the differences Lawrence has experienced,
this root contrast between men and animals is the
one he brings out best. In an early book, describing
someone looking at an anemone in a rock pool, he
says: 'He had to get a sense of the anemone and a
sympathetic knowledge of its experience into his
blood, before he was satisfied.'

Suddenly, in the midst of descriptions of disintegration, or the horrors of doing good to the masses,
or the principle of aristocracy, comes a passage
about some animal – often in one of the essays –
like this:

> The carrion birds, aristocrats, sit up high and remote, on
> the sterile rocks of the old absolute, their obscene heads
> gripped hard and small, like knots of stone clenched upon
> themselves for ever.

Some people make a distinction between 'wild'
animals, which they distantly admire, and 'domestic,'
which they own and perhaps therefore patronise.

Lawrence *owns* his cat ('with forward-thrusting
bolts of white paws') and his cow too, but he has
seen too much to patronise. He has seen his cow —
'swinging across the field, snatching off the tops of
the little wild sunflowers as if she were mowing.
And down they go, down her black throat. And
when she stands in her cowy oblivion chewing her
cud, with her lower jaw swinging peacefully, and I
am milking her, suddenly the camomiley smell of
her breath, as she glances round with glaring,
smoke-blue eyes . . .' and so on, to the point of
the essay (it is about the Principle of Destruction).

His Cow? 'My cow Susan is at my disposal
indeed. But when I see her suddenly emerging,
jet-black, sliding through the gate of her little corral
into the open sun, does not my heart stand still,
and cry out, in some long-forgotten tongue, saluta-
tion to the fearsome one?'

The most difficult thing Lawrence seems to
succeed in is his attempt to give the feeling of these
other animal worlds existing in a kind of arbitrary
contemporaneousness with our own. He is able,
in some degree, to describe animals in terms of
themselves. The world of the doe:

'. . . She
put back her fine, level-balanced head.
And I knew her.

Ah yes, being male, is not my head
hard-balanced, antlered?
Are not my haunches light?'

The world of the carrion animals:

'The hyæna can scarcely see and hear the living
world; it draws back on to the stony fixity of its
own loins, draws back upon its own nullity, sightless
save for carrion. The vulture can neither see nor
hear the living world, it is one supreme glance, the
glance in search of carrion, its own absolute quench-
ing, beyond which is nothing.'

The world of the fish:

'Your life a sluice of sensation along your
sides. . . .
No fingers, no hands and feet, no lips:
No tender muzzles,
No wistful bellies. . . .

Quelle joie de vivre
Dans l'eau!
Slowly to gape through the waters. . . .
They are beyond me, are fishes.
I stand at the pale of my being
And look beyond. . . .

THE QUALITY OF THE UNCONSCIOUS. All these qualities and distinctions could be described together
under one heading: they are all connected in some

way with what is called 'the unconscious.' The
difficulty of talking about consciousness or uncon-
sciousness is that amusing ignorance or depressing
knowledge of technical metaphysical terms may be
betrayed. To talk of a 'philosophy of the unconscious' seems almost a contradiction. Such philosophies — psycho-analysis, of course, included[1] — are
all the result of the developing consciousness of men,
more and more able to specify, as new territory is
added, what is conscious and what is unconscious
in us. Lawrence's own era is exemplified in him in
this respect, that his *action* is on the line of self-
knowledge. He records this partly by setting forth
the new qualities he finds there, in the unrealised
part of himself. But besides this the fact that he
himself has gone a short way into an unknown
country has given him an idea of its extent. He
wants to emphasise, therefore, how 'the unconscious' is the most powerful force working behind
the events in his books. He shows this chiefly, but
not only, by making real wants unaffected by superficial wishes. He is always writing, too, of the
unconscious differences which seasons, times of day,

[1] Judging from the *Encyclopædia Britannica* and references to Lawrence
in one or two American lecture courses on the modern English Novel,
Lawrence is officially regarded as the Novelist of Psycho-analysis. But
though Lawrence sometimes uses its terminology, the point of his books
will be missed if they are interpreted on the pathological basis of a science
which puts 'infantile experience' in the position of the Fates and Furies
of classical tragedy and makes it, with its power of deciding events before
they have happened, as fatal to dramatic interest as any *deus ex machina*.
Power over their own fates, or perhaps power to abandon themselves to
their fates, is an essential implication behind the life of his characters.

latitudes, make on a man. From his own life he can show how each different part of the world can draw something new out of whoever can submit to its hidden influence. Each different continent of the world has its own demons, which can put a man, if he will allow, into some positive productive connection with the country he is in. But these powers can only be assimilated in the blood: they have no validity to him who is determined to put his finger on them and 'follow Nature.' As Nietzsche says 'according to Nature! Oh, you noble stoics, what fraud of words! Imagine to yourselves, beings like Nature, boundlessly extravagant, boundlessly indifferent, without purpose or consideration, without pity or justice, at once fruitful, barren, and uncertain: imagine to yourselves *indifference* as a power — how could you live in accordance with such indifference!'

In his criticism, Lawrence makes his Satans men who deny the undiscovered world, or who represent it by a neat creed. As he says in his essay on Benjamin Franklin (criticising his attempt to draw up beliefs which would 'satisfy the professors of every religion, but shock none'): 'the soul of man is a vast forest, and all Benjamin intended was a neat back garden . . . who knows what will come out of the soul of man? The soul of man is a dark vast forest, with wild life in it.'

Part of Lawrence's feelings about the dark races, or about animals, lies in the fact that the free working of their unconscious motives is less trammelled by the renascence Hamlet's capacities for 'thinking too precisely on the event.'

Dostoievsky novels are full of this kind of self-frustration. 'I am a louse,' Raskolnikov says of the murder, 'I am a louse, because not for my own fleshly lusts did I undertake it, but with a grand and noble object.' He let his determinations go against his unconscious needs – a kind of self-overlapping which, Lawrence would imply, comes from denying the wants of the 'unconscious' – most hidden but most formidable because nearest the stream of life.

THE GOD QUALITY. Move these attributes of Lawrence another half-turn round and they are joined in yet another new and entirely different implication. All that has been said so far means, in effect, that he sees more in things than meets the eye. What is this less than seeing the God part of things – the knowing of the quality of God in them?

To speak in this way is to define God as something which all creative artists experience when they demonstrate, by example of creation, the infinite possible crystallisations which lie behind the pre-conceived forms and predetermined characters of things and people. Lawrence, by being a poet, reveals God in that sense; yet there is a certain important difference between the man who shows God in this concrete if nameless manner, and the

man who uses the word 'God,' who puts the fact
of God obviously and separately in his work, as
Lawrence sometimes does.

Recently Lawrence has constantly been writing
about God. That he should do this more than he
does in his earlier books is not due to any fundamental change in himself but to the development of
a proselytising tendency. He believes himself to
be living in a world where God is suppressed.
Nowhere was this more obviously the case, he
thought, than among the clear-minded, common-
sense inhabitants of the world of Christianity-
without-miracles which he was brought up to. A
world which had as its background a common-sense
science, with no belief in the metaphysical reality of
man; a world which liked to indulge in calm pathological explanations of people or cool 'discoveries'
of the structure of objects or the shape of dimensions
— as if what was explained or discovered had been
there all the time — all without any acknowledgment
of the existence of other universes besides the
scientific one of which it is a part.

Perhaps the psychologies of suppression contained a metaphor of the truth. The libido is suppressed, one says. On the contrary, chastity is
suppressed, say ascetic counterblasts. Or glands
are starved. Perhaps the image of suppression,
of lack of flow, represents a god suppression which
afflicts us.

Lawrence certainly thinks so. Probably the only
criticism of his work which he would listen to now

would be on this very aspect, whether or not it had something of God in it.

Talk about religion? 'I reckon a crow is religious when he sails across the sky,' says Paul Morel. Nevertheless Lawrence has chosen to set forth his gods. To describe, in particular, his dark god. To write *The Plumed Serpent* and explain a religion. To construct a theogony and forms of worship. Is it that the experience of apprehension has been so vivid in him that he wants to give a name to it? That he wants to make sure of guarding against failure to allow of its repetition? That he wants to lead other people into that experience?

To many, there will appear most of God in his work when he is describing, in his special way, below the surface. Or when he is applying to men his criterion – not the black category and the white category but his real criterion, the question Are they obeyers of life? Do they allow their life to flow on its course? Are they 'Answerers'?

Lawrence has a horror of holding back. Perhaps he recognises a tendency to withhold something in himself: he describes with striking truth this kind of struggle. Lady Daphne in *The Ladybird*. Should she break away from the unnatural, forced life which was destroying her? She looks at herself in the glass.

> . . . Never! She always caught herself back . . . at the very thought of that relaxation some hypersensitive nerve started with a great twinge in her breast.

To Lawrence the knowledge of God is largely this ability not to hold back, not to say 'I think it would be going rather too far.' A curious belief of salvation in abandonment; but abandonment, really, to obedience; obedience to life.

PART FOUR
SOME CONCLUSIONS

SOME CONCLUSIONS

LAWRENCE THE KEY TO HIS PHILOSOPHY. In the light of what has so far been said of him, it is possible to say something more about the Lawrence 'gist' which was the subject of the first part of the book. A man who, in giving his views, demonstrates their meaning with strong images, illustrates them in many concrete examples, and expands them without too much consistency — such a man is doing more than presenting ideas: he is describing a person. As self-description, Lawrence 'gist' at once takes on a value which can only be understood, nevertheless, in the light of the rest of what he writes.

THE ANTAGONIST OF 'SEX.' This is most obviously true when Lawrence is talking about sexual experience. The sexual experience is the most difficult to translate into words and therefore most invincibly exists in our minds in the form of preconception. Yet because of its importance to him it is just this kind of experience which Lawrence has had to try to describe.

'Obedience to life.' Life utters certain commands. To some, for instance, it says: 'Follow the impulse to chastity.' To others: 'Follow the impulse to procreation.' It is this impulse which has impelled Lawrence — to create, by means of the self renewal which comes in the train of the act of successful sexual consummation.

Before he could set forth an individual experience of it, Lawrence characteristically felt the necessity for saying forcibly what, to him, it did *not* mean. He does this, in effect, by attacking 'sex.'

'Sex' is the brief confident word round which all the sex ideas parade. For instance: that there are things connected with sex which can be scientifically observed and disinterestedly examined. That the field of human knowledge can be made richer by the study of germ cells and the comparison of the homologous sexual characteristics of animals. That the sum of human happiness can be enlarged by the systematisation of birth-control or the logical practise of eugenics. That there is sexual indulgence. That sexual intercourse is a device for producing children. That the libido is god. That there is a simple and natural way of 'telling children all about it' that is beneficial: conversely that 'coarse talk' is injurious. That sex is beautiful. That sex is ugly. Such ideas, and many steadfast theories, belong to the word 'sex.'

Lawrence thinks: — as if anyone could tell anyone all about it. Or as if coarse little boys were any more wrong or any more right than the nice mother or the learned scientist. This kind of 'sex' does not describe sexual experience. It implies that the acts and passions of procreation exist all by themselves cut off from everything else. This cannot be experience.

Not only has Lawrence to put himself outside the various preconceptions of sex: there are the classical ways of writing about it. One of these Lawrence attacks specifically — the romantic and pure way, *du bist wie eine blume*, bound to be accompanied, he thinks, by the desire to tell private smoking-room stories. What are the other classical approaches? Complementary to the last there is the openly cynical way, the Restoration dramatist, witty and fashionable way correspondingly likely, perhaps, to be supplemented by secret leanings towards what is pure and lofty. Then there is the dry, the sly, the humorous way, the Shaw and Butler way, treating sex as an amusing weakness. Then there is misogyny. Then there are those who write calmly, clearly, and 'nicely' about it — the mothercraft way, or those who write calmly, clearly, scientifically.

Lawrence, a young man in the age of realistic or scientific sex treatment, has various positive experiences connected with coition he is naturally anxious shall not be confused with any of these views or ways of writing, which he therefore attacks.

He attacks psycho-analysis, because it sees the sexual motive as the one and only motive. To make it the only motive means to make it God. He attacks the 'chemical analysis,' which he says is 'just a farce' (he begs the question, for militant purposes, whether all science is not farcical if interpreted in terms of what is not science). Then he attacks the 'no nonsense' methods of modern coeducation and familiarity between the sexes. 'The nice clean intimacy which we now so admire between the sexes is sterilising,' he says. 'It makes neuters. Later on, no deep, magical sex-life is possible.' Then: 'Sex should come upon us a terrible thing of suffering and privilege and mystery.' So, says Lawrence to mothers, don't instruct thus: 'You see, dear, one day you'll love a man as I love Daddy . . . and then, dear, I hope you'll marry him. Because if you do you'll be happy, and I want you to be happy, my love. And so I hope you'll marry the man you really love (kisses the child).'

Don't do this either, he says. 'It is wrong to make sex appear as if it were part of the spiritual love. It is even worse to take the scientific test-tube line. It all kills the great effective dynamism of life, and substitutes the mere ash of mental ideas and tricks.'

It is much better, he says, never to talk about sex. The whole subject is so talked about and thought about that it is all raised to the spiritual plane, to the upper half of the body, where it all belongs. The whole race, Lawrence implies as he warms to it, is suffering from sex in the head; so that so far as complete and fully experienced consummation is concerned we are impotent. Sex must be forgotten for a generation.

> Leave sex alone.
> Sex is a state of grace
> and you'll have to wait.

Lawrence has more positive things to say about it than this — but the very fact that he has so much to write makes him angry to find some of his metaphors already hackneyed by people who have no right of experience to use them.

His own way is like no one else's. First of all, he writes less of the delicate preliminaries and skirmishes that sometimes precede the act than the converging streams beneath the surface which draw the two people together. Coition itself he describes again and again — never generalising, each time taking a different kind of pairing and showing the different experience possible in each. Yet though each is different, whether he is writing of a man or a woman there is always the sense of great sweeping motions. ('The passion came up in him, stroke after stroke, like the ringing of a bronze bell.') The being carried away on this flood.

He gives his knowledge more freely in these passages than anywhere else. An exception, perhaps, is *Lady Chatterley's Lover*, where the meticulous going over of every detail, of every word and thought connected with the subject, reminds one of the attempts of lesser men to escape from a non-conformist education. There is something of a self-purge about it — especially in the light of a poem in the subsequent *Pansies* about 'Lady C.' when he says to his wife: 'Don't you feel glad now I wrote it? You were angry — but don't you feel the better for it?' Why better? Yet in *Lady Chatterley* there are many passages recalling various phases and species

of the sexual experience which are very good indeed.
An extraordinary speech, for instance, where the
gamekeeper goes over his past sexual life, and shows
how the varying characters, the depth or shallow-
ness of the women, affected the consummation.
And the fully described contrast between Lady
Chatterley's experience with Mellors and with the
other man, the exaggeratedly civilised man.

Lawrence puts a powerful 'ought' to this. First,
that 'ought' should not come in, that there should
be no sex *determination*. ('Rarely use venery but for
health and off-spring': – Benjamin Franklin. 'On
the contrary *never* "use" venery': – Lawrence.)
Then – the real implication of 'sex' should be that
it is part of something greater. In Lawrence it leads
on, itself, to something greater. It is only preparatory, 'a consummation in darkness preparatory to a
new journey towards consummation in spirit.' It
implies that deep as the sexual motives are, there are
other motives deeper and more extensive, and others
deeper and more extensive than these again.

A LAWRENCE CRITERION. The life-theory part of
Lawrence is more frequent in the essays, but it is
neither less vivid nor less unscientific there. Theory,
in fact, is at a disadvantage in the novels. He
attempts to dramatise it, to make its way of being
stated fit the characters. Lawrence-views on Thomas
Hardy spoken in a foreign accent by a leader of a
circus troup (*The Lost Girl*). Or the Lawrence-man

in the novels becomes a sort of grave humorous silent person never saying anything that isn't profound, slightly detestable sometimes, like Lilley in *Aaron's Rod*. There are people, too, you are meant to agree with, and others which you are meant to see are on the wrong track.

Perhaps this section should be called Lawrence As Critic. Some of the essays are about other writers — Galsworthy, Melville, Poe, Tolstoy — but they are not critical in the sense that he suddenly switches over and writes in a critical scientific way. 'Criticism can never be a science,' he says, 'it is, in the first place, much too personal, and in the second, it is concerned with values that science ignores. The touchstone is emotion, not reason.' By 'emotion' he means feeling,[1] and feeling of the kind which can only be aroused by something which itself feels — which is living.

In effect there is in this one criterion. Lawrence only discusses writers who succeed, half succeed, or instructively fail to reveal life.

For instance, he will ask of a man's action: Does it establish a new connection between mankind and the universe, 'resulting in a vast release of energy, as the work of Voltaire, Shelley, Wordsworth, Byron or Rousseau does?'

---

[1] 'A critic must be able to *feel* the impact of a work of art in all its complexity and force. To do so, he must be a man of force and complexity himself, which few critics are. A man with a paltry, impudent nature will never write anything but paltry, impudent criticism. And a man who is *emotionally* educated is rare as a phœnix. The more scholastically educated a man is generally, the more he is an emotional boor.'

Or else: Does a man put power into the world? 'It may be Newton's Law or Cæsar's Rome or Jesus' Christianity or even Attila's charred ruins. . . . Something new displaces something old, and sometimes room has to be cleared beforehand.' Writers are valuable even if, like Edgar Allen Poe, they sincerely express the doom of our way of life (the doom of the white race). This is what Herman Melville is describing in *Moby Dick* (our doom symbolically embodied in the death of the white whale). Even the satirist, 'by ridiculing the social being,' can 'help the true individual, the real human being, to rise to his feet again.' Nevertheless there should be a positive side to the satire, and this must not be merely a mechanically constructed antithesis of the thing attacked. Like Galsworthy, for instance, who would have written a great satire on the Social way to death, on Forsytism, if he hadn't set up as his Positive emancipated-passion people like Irene and the gentlemanly lusters like Bosinney — anti-Forsytes. Lawrence does not care for Galsworthy on sex, Galsworthy wanting to make it the Positive. 'He wants to make it important, and he only makes it repulsive.'

There are few *living* English writers living, in Lawrence's estimation. I believe he thinks well of E. M. Forster. *Passage to India* is a good commentary on the hostility between the Indian and white ways of consciousness.

Hardy, however perfectly he may express the love of earth, treats in his main situations of an old and

futile world. The Tess situation belongs to an old
world, and has only a trivial kind of significance.

These opinions of Lawrence are often put down
in the novels, in a miscellaneous way, or in poems:

'When I read Shakespeare I am struck with
wonder that such trivial people should muse and
thunder in such lovely language.'

Of the stock modern writers, he says: 'All of
them, when it comes to their philosophy, or what
they think-they-are, they are all crucified Jesuses.
. . . *Lord Jim, Sylvestre Bonnard. If Winter
Comes, Main Street, Ulysses, Pan* . . . they are all
pathetic or sympathetic or antipathetic little Jesuses
accomplis or *manqués*.'

When it comes to their philosophy, Lawrence
says – meaning that they may express a great deal
outside their own misinterpretations of their experience. But the fact is that all considerable
novelists 'have a didactic purpose, otherwise a
philosophy, directly opposed to their passional
inspiration.' The general scheme of the essays in
Classical American Literature is the separation of
what he believes to be unreal fabricated scheme
from 'passional inspiration.' This must always be
worth doing, but Lawrence's plan has this limitation,
that he cannot count as 'passionate' a philosophy
the general trend of which is different from his own.
At heart, he says of them, they are all phallic wor-
shippers. Therefore they are all false to themselves
– Tolstoy with his Christian socialism, Whitman

with his universal love, Plato with his smoothness and revulsion away from the earth, Wordsworth with his seeing in nature something lofty and pure. Even Dante, with his worship of a remote Beatrice, when all the time he had 'a cosy bifurcated wife in his bed, and a family of lusty little Dantinos.' Lawrence's god is a jealous god.

Lawrence is not writing critically — it is the general taste of the philosophy of these writers he does not care for. Though he gives them recognition, it is not for their god, opposed to his own. His one criterion is where, *for him*, they increase life — release new life.

ANTI LAWRENCE.

i. A note on 'obsession.'

'Extraordinary freshness — dynamic power,' reviewers used to repeat over the group of novels which came out soon after the war, 'if only it were not for the unfortunate obsessions.' Well, there is nothing surprising in that being said of Lawrence. What, however, were the instances? He was always considered to be obsessed by *sex*. Running the primitive races and the unconscious as well, but above all sex.

Yet new sides of that very mode of experience was what he felt most strongly he had to write about. What man can over-demonstrate new manifestations he is trying to add to life — new true statements? No — no, of course he under expresses — everyone must. Everyone must be still too bound to the accepted description to bring out fully an individual meaning. Of course he is always trying new ways to make his creation his own. This is not obsession.

Nevertheless there is an atmosphere of obsession. A man is obsessed by whatever he has allowed himself to bring only partially to the conscious plane. By something which he has allowed to remain as it were stuck in his gullet, half in darkness, and half in the full light of conscious acceptance. There is often, in Lawrence, a hint of something being held back. When he writes about sex it seems as if there was a clue withheld, in Lawrence's own life or in what he says about it. Since sex is one of the chief directions of Lawrence's action, he should be able to illustrate his theme infinitely. Sometimes he seems to keep to one aspect of it too long. It is because he does not go far enough; that is why sometimes he seems overemphatic.

The atmosphere of obsession more obviously surrounds what he says of the world of 'white idealism' which he seems to be trying not so much to apprehend as to get away from. There is obsession here, and much of Lawrence's work is under the shadow of this struggle, meaningless and unnecessary to some. But this drawback always belongs to iconoclasm.

ii. The special limitation of iconoclasts.

'Men live,' Lawrence says, 'according to some gradually developing and gradually withering vision.

And at present there is too much of an outworn vision.'

Too much of an outworn vision. It is always true to say that of mankind, though not of persons. There are sometimes individuals who are able to stigmatise the old way of living and clear the ground for a new one – the lions of Nietzsche's second metamorphosis. But to appreciate the destructive-ness of these lions you must yourself be feeling fierce. You must yourself have an appetite for the lamb to be devoured – in this case the white and emasculated lamb of common-sense Christianity. Your own blood must have been impregnated, as Lawrence's was in his youth, with the particular kind of idealism which, like Lawrence, you must be angrily wanting to work out of the system: otherwise his attacks will all seem unnecessary.

For this is the limitation of iconoclasm, that it is inseparable from the old way of life which it wants to break. Lawrence is tied to the barren country he is besieging; when he is making war on his old environment he is still kowtowing to it in point of fact. His readers may want to forget such things and walk away. Lawrence is really kowtowing to it, and in so doing seems to acquire some of the faults of the idealism he is attacking. Limited by his method, he tends to set up the ideal of the opposite and this, the least important part of his Positive, naturally tends to become a kind of Movement, furthering the elevation of the general level of man-kind with the help of a new ideal. Lawrence wants to give coal miners picturesque red trousers, tied up round the ankles like the Mexicans.[1] Only idealists write satire.

iii. The Lawrence Manner.

Among literary critics Lawrence's name has dubious prestige. Edith Sitwell calls him the Jaeger poet.

The reasons for this are numerous, obvious, and insurmountable.

The only general charge brought against him of significance in an unliterary judgment is connected with the many 'lapses in style' and prolixities of which he is accused.[2]

Lawrence, in the superficial part of his character, was, and is, a romantic young man. Being 'romantic' means obedience to the commandment 'I ought to feel deeply.' Being 'classical' means obedience to: 'I ought to feel deeply about art.' When Lawrence is writing badly or slackly, from whatever cause, he is inclined to stand by this first rule, taking no notice of the second. The effect is that suddenly, in the middle of some magnificent novel, will come two or three pages of rank writing, pure novelese. I do not mean a certain anti-intellectual roughness of style, which he assumes quite successfully, nor his too frequent tendency to repeat key words – often with

[1] *Lady Chatterley.*

[2] I once heard Max Beerbohm say of Lawrence's introduction to Maurice Magnus' *Memoirs* : 'Pages and pages of *stuff* – which an *artist* could have done in twenty paragraphs.'

K

great effect — nor his way of beginning almost every mid-paragraph sentence with 'And' or 'But.' That belongs to the realms of style. It is when he coldly writes pure novelese.

The White Peacock was a first book. It is natural that things like 'all the glamour of our yesterdays' and 'weaving him into the large magic of the years' should be fairly frequent. But in *Sons and Lovers*, a mature novel, Lawrence sometimes sinks down to nothing and this kind of writing rises in his place: 'The naked hunger and inevitability of his loving her, something strong and blind and ruthless in its primitiveness. . . . She did this for him in his need.' Even in the best books, *Women in Love* for instance, the Lawrence hero will say to the Lawrence heroine that he 'feels as if he could just meet her, and they would set off, just towards the distance'; so that we are not surprised when they do start off, in a motor-car in the dark, that the distance appears 'magic and elfin.' Probably the heroine was feeling, like Alvina Houghton in *The Lost Girl*, that 'for the time being she was all dark and potent.' Well — as Coleridge says, speaking in his Dr. Johnson manner: 'Poetry ought not to have always its highest relish.'

PRO LAWRENCE. This century there have been many clever and profound philosophers and theorists who cannot only express what they want to say but who are definitely something more than academic philo-

sophers, most of them strongly antagonistic to such
philosophy on the grounds that it is divorced from
experience, themselves men of action and living
unacademic lives. Men who are emphatically not
philosophers only but ethical philosophers like
William James, mathematical philosophers like
Whitehead, psychologist philosophers like Havelock Ellis, physicist philosophers like Eddington,
brilliant journalist philosophers like Sullivan; and
Bergson, and now Keyserling.

The modern young man says: Which must I
read? In the past, the answer to the question seems
usually to have been fairly obvious. No one, living
in Germany in 1780, can have doubted that it must
be Goethe – or in France, a hundred years later, that
it was Rousseau. But nowadays no sooner does one
man establish himself than he is knocked down by
his successor. Shaw is out of date, of course.
Lawrence has for ever got rid of him by implication.
Anyhow Jung would have explained him by the
simplest diagnosis – Freud rather. Remember
Freud? But Lawrence is all in Spengler – read
Spengler. And Spengler has been going for ages
in Germany – Vaihinger has been much more read
on the Continent for years. And do you know that
Spengler doesn't even mention Einstein – of course,
he regards him as belonging to the finishing stage
of the *old* mathematic, the old departing mathematic; certainly not as a forerunner of anything
new. And anyhow Whitehead has in effect put
Weyl behind his back who put Einstein behind *his*

back years ago.[1] So that you get writers like Wyndham Lewis who gravely stand by ready to bang on the head anybody who opens his mouth. Perfectly logical and right.

Yet it is bewildering for the Young Man. How shall I keep up? he says. Which can I most safely leave out? This is the general attitude now among those who want to lose everything in a kind of passion of being up to the mark: an attitude not much different from that of an unhappy nervous woman catching a train. She unconsciously causes herself to be late so that she may be made blind and deaf to everything but the idea of train catching, of being up to time. Pre-occupied by this lust she is completely indifferent even to the curious recesses of the taxi interior, or the expressive skin of the back of the taxi-driver's neck.

It is difficult not to be affected by this way of thinking. Why is it that when we read in history regretful records of the fact that Francis Bacon took no notice of Copernicus, Galileo jealously ignored Kepler, Kant wouldn't read Fichte, we think it was a great pity? It must all be the result of a tendency to lay the emphasis on the theory, the metaphysic of the writer rather than on the new apprehension of the world from which the metaphysic is deduced. It is the result, also, of a tendency in the writers themselves to bring the rest of their work into line with their philosophy, to make the rest of their work an illustration of it.

[1] I cannot guarantee these facts.

Is it in unphilosophical writing – poetry – 'literature' that new worlds of individual expression will be found least obscured? Here again huge barriers will often be discovered constructed by the author between himself and his readers. In English literature, where the barriers are mostly of the same kind, it is the standard writers who most effectively conceal themselves – Tennyson, Arnold, Spenser, Meredith, Chaucer, all the essay writers, most modern verse writers, who all get behind, at times, such charming bulwarks as humour; a regular sweetness; freshness in simplicity; rough 'realism' of the soil, beer, meat and country life (– all highly idealised); whimsicality; picture of a man who, detached from ugly things, contemplates beauty; man of sensibility who leaves certain things unspoken – all so many cloaks and so many disguises inside which the writer himself is hidden and only appears (when there is anyone there at all) between the folds, and by chance, at rare intervals. If explanation obstructs our sight of philosophic writers, the literariness of unphilosophical ones at times obscures them altogether.

To some, Lawrence seems one of the English writers who succeeds in revealing. He is neither fresh, nor simple, and there is no steady humour in his work. One of his characteristics is a heavy sensuousness of description, a rough way of expressing his meaning by piling extreme on extreme. There is no economy, no restraint. But whether such ways of writing commend themselves or not, they do not especially tend to conceal the man who uses them.

Lawrence reveals; though not in any special characteristic, nor even in the Birkins, but in all the ingredients taken together – in his coldness towards well-groomed men . . . description of tin cans merging into undergrowth in an Australian suburb . . . penetrating attack on America . . . seeing himself as Lilley or R. L. Somers . . . description of a mare trying to get at a stallion . . . making his heroes say 'Nay' when they contradict his heroines . . . theory of ganglia . . . compassionate creation of Jack, 'The Boy in the Bush' . . . bit of Biblical prose . . . rough and ready account of a maternity nurse's apprenticeship in London . . . word of marvellous descriptiveness . . . frustrated annoyance at his own presence in the same world with cold English good-breeding . . . disliking women who say 'You do love me, darling, don't you?' . . . knowledge of the feel of a small bird standing in the palm of his hand 'with almost weightless feet' . . . coming assertively round to doctrine at the end of a chapter . . . marvellously making doctrine and description all one in a chapter on crucifixes in Northern Italy . . . unintellectually calling Tolstoy 'old Leo.'

It is such characteristics taken together with the qualities which have been already partly described which go to make the Lawrence world, a world capable of enriching, in separate and different ways, the separate and different worlds of his readers.

In his later books, Lawrence seems to want to lead, to be a leader of a kind of community of 'real' aristocrats. We can imagine his typical Young Man reader saying: 'Well, Mr. Lawrence, you won't lead me – and you would never want to, because I am tall and fair and blue-eyed and white-race Nordic for one thing, and besides, I am educated and civilised and conscious, and constantly trying in many ways to become more so. Nevertheless you have influenced me as I want to be influenced. You have strengthened the current of the main stream of my life, so that there is less stagnating on the margins, you have released into life something which was frozen before. You have influenced me, I say, in the way I want to be influenced.'

On the whole, the Young Man feels antagonistic: his admiration is deep, but grudging. It seems as if an appreciation of Lawrence must always be made in a half-antagonistic way. Perhaps the reason is that conflict is what he himself best expresses. His first essay was called *The Crown*; but in spite of *The Plumed Serpent*, his subject is not really the crown, the prize, but the antagonists who are fighting for it. The lion, and the unicorn. A continual metaphor of his own struggle, first to be and then to know himself. A momentous attempt to learn, by living, to *be*, and to learn, by living, to *know*, is what the autobiography of Lawrence discloses. Criticisms will in the future be made of the way in which often, during the ups and downs of the fight, he urges precepts opposed to this example. Learn not to know, he says in his attacks on idealism or the intellect — and, in effect, learn to be not yourself but someone different.

Criticisms again — and yet it is to Lawrence I owe my greatest debt. To me and to many thousands he is the great living writer of this generation, who has had the power, in a sense which separates him from all his contemporaries, to create a world.

I had arranged to go to Bandol to try to see Lawrence for the first time, making this book the excuse, when he was taken ill and died. It was known that he had been kept in his room most of the bad, rainy winter with asthma and bronchitis, yet few of his English friends took seriously the reports of his health which were printed a few days before his death.

But for years Lawrence had lived chiefly by the resistance and impetus of his vitality; he should, medically speaking, have died long ago. Those who know Lawrence through his work will believe that in some way his death coincided with the completion of his activity, or at any rate with a period of activity. That though he must have continued to fight against death, there must have been the knowledge in him somewhere that his addition to the world had been established — that his new action had been expressed. That then, perhaps, something in him turned to accept death. At once came the merciful final stage of his disease.

'The spotted hawk swoops by and accuses me,
    he complains of my gab and my loitering . . .
The last scud of day holds back for me. . . .'

The finishing stanza of the *Song of Myself*, beginning with these lines, makes, I think, a good epitaph.

APPENDIX

LIST OF THE PRINCIPAL PUBLICATIONS OF D. H. LAWRENCE

Extracts from E. D. McDonald's 'Bibliography,'
Philadelphia, 1925

*

i. 'A youthful story in the bad grey print of a provincial newspaper — under a *nom de plume.* But, thank God, that has gone to glory in the absolute sense.'

ii. Poems (e.g. 'A Still Afternoon', 'Dreams Old and Nascent', begin to be published in the *English Review,* November 1909).

iii. First short story, 'Goose Fair', in the *English Review,* February 1910.

*

1. *The White Peacock,* a novel   Jan. 1911
2. *The Trespasser,* a novel   May 1912
3. *Love Poems and Others*   Feb. 1913
   Began to appear June 1912, *Saturday Westminster Gazette.*
4. *Sons and Lovers,* a novel   May 1913
5. *The Widowing of Mrs. Holroyd,* a play Apr. 1914
6. *The Prussian Officer and Other Stories* Dec. 1914
   Began to appear February 1910
7. *The Rainbow,* a novel   Sept. 1915

8. *The Crown*, an essay published in the three numbers of *The Signature*, Oct. 4th, 18th, and Nov. 4th. The only other contributors to this paper, which came to an end with the third number, were Katherine Mansfield and J. Middleton Murry   1915

9. *Amores*, poems   July 1916
Began to appear 1909.

10. *Twilight in Italy*, essays   June 1916
Began to appear March 1912.

11. *Look! We Have Come Through*, a sequence of poems written 1912–17   Dec. 1917

12. *New Poems.*   Oct. 1918
Began to appear 1910

13. *Bay*, poems   Nov. 1919

14. *Touch and Go*, a play   May 1920

15. *Women in Love*, a novel   Nov. 1920
Written in 1916

16. *The Lost Girl*, a novel   Nov. 1920

17. *Psycho-analysis and the Unconscious*   May 1921

18. *Tortoises*, poems   Dec. 1921

19. *Sex and Sardinia*, essays   Dec. 1921

20. *Aaron's Rod*, a novel   April 1922

21. *Fantasia of the Unconscious*, essays   Oct. 1922

22. *England, My England*, short stories   Oct. 1922

23. *The Ladybird*, long-short stories   March 1923

24. *Studies in Classic American Literature*   Aug. 1923

25. *Kangaroo*, a novel   Sept. 1923

26. *Birds, Beasts and Flowers*, poems   Oct. 1923
Including *Tortoises*.

27. *The Boy in the Bush*, a novel   Aug. 1924

28. Introduction to Maurice Magnus' *Memoirs
    of the Foreign Legion*   1924
29. *St. Maur*, three stories   1925
30. *The Plumed Serpent*, a novel   1926
31. *David*, a play   1926
32. *Mornings in Mexico*, essays   1927
33. *The Woman Who Rode Away*, long-short
    stories   1928
34. *Lady Chatterley's Lover*, a novel   1928
35. *Pansies*, poems   1929

NOTE

In answer to a question, Mr. Lawrence wrote: 'I believe my books are published pretty well in the order in which they were written: I don't think there are any serious divergencies. Only *Women in Love* was finished by end of 1916, and didn't get published till some years later—was it 1922? I haven't got any important unprinted works: and I don't think any exist.' (Letter dated January 9th, 1930.)